Praise

"This book is meant to be savored. Sip on a chapter, contemplate, let it float around your subconscious and discover the truth of the lesson in your soul. It's reminiscent of Dr. Wayne Dyer's *Change Your Thoughts—Change Your Life: Living the Wisdom of the Tao* with the difference being that *Sitting on the Toolbox* uses stories to slide the lesson under the subconscious."
    – MIKI STRONG, Creator, PERSONA Branding Archetypes

"Turn to any page and you'll find a relevant question, a real-life example, an entertaining story, or a mindful Buddhist practice that could change your life. That's the simple magic of this wonderful book. While it's easy to pick up, it's hard to put down. Keep this literal loving-kindness toolbox nearby. That way, you can open it and grab profound wisdom and practical advice to fill you with joy at any time."
    – MARY GUSTAFSON, Author, *My Wish: The Story of a Man Who Brought Happiness to America*

"*Sitting on the Toolbox* by Venerable Bhante Sujatha and Stacey Stern is full of deep wisdom from a spiritual master. You can feel compassion, warmth, and ease coming off the page. But what makes this book so special is how down-to-earth the teachings are. Bhante meets his readers and students at our level. This is a beautiful book."
    – BRAD WETZLER, Journalist, Author, and Founder, Yoga of Writing

"*Sitting on the Toolbox* is a treasure chest of uplifting, compassionate, and practical wisdom I was able to apply immediately to practice loving-kindness to others—and myself. Through captivating stories and brilliant analogies, I was brought to laughter and tears on the path to discovering the beauty in everything, even while being aware of the pain. *Sitting on the Toolbox* is definitely going into my personal toolbox of guides to living a joyful life."

– MARIAN HEAD, Author, *Revolutionary Agreements: A Personal Path to Peace on Earth*

"This monk has taught me one thing above all others. Do not bother learning any wisdom from any of the great wisdom teachers unless you commit to putting that wisdom into your daily actions. Make wisdom visible, palpable, like a garland draped all over your life. *Sitting on the Toolbox* is a simple and straightforward instruction manual, a how-to on applying wisdom to make your world, thereby the whole world, better. Make this your morning devotional . . . take one tool and use it every day. If you do, I guarantee sturdy happiness as a result."

– TYLER LEWKE, President, Blue Lotus Buddhist Temple, and Author, *Empty, Empty. Happy, Happy: The Essential Teachings of a Simple Monk*

Sitting on the Toolbox
Buddha's Wisdom for a Joyful Life

VENERABLE BHANTE SUJATHA
with STACEY STERN

Blue Lotus Press
Woodstock, IL 60098
www.sittingonthetoolbox.com

First print edition published in 2018

Book cover design by Jessica Dunegan
Interior layout and design by Hynek Palatin
Proofreading by Amber Byers of Tadpole Press
Photo of Venerable Bhante Sujatha by Chathura Jayasinghe
Photo of Stacey Stern by Shari Regenbogen Ross

Publisher's Cataloging-in-Publication Data
Names: Sujatha, Bhante, Venerable, 1967-, author. | Stern, Stacey,
     1966-, author.
Title: Sitting on the toolbox: Buddha's wisdom for a joyful life /
     Venerable Bhante Sujatha with Stacey Stern.
Description: First print edition. | Woodstock, IL : Blue Lotus Press,
     2018. | Summary: Buddhist monk Venerable Bhante Sujatha uses
     humor, personal anecdotes, and a mix of ancient and modern
     stories to show you how to access your own deep truths and live
     a fuller, more joyful life.
Identifiers: LCCN 2018911462 | ISBN 9781732775800
Subjects: LCSH: Happiness—Religious aspects—Buddhism. | Spiritual
     life— Buddhism. | BISAC: SELF-HELP / Personal Growth /
     Happiness | BODY, MIND & SPIRIT / Inspiration & Personal
     Growth | RELIGION / Buddhism / General.
Classification: LCC BQ4570.J69.S85 | DDC 294.3/444—dc23
LC record available at http://lccn.loc.gov/2018911462

For Buddha and all the teachers who have guided us

Contents

PART THREE

Drilling Deeper: Moving from surviving to thriving

Mindfulness

Joy

Sponsors

We bow deeply in gratitude to the following sponsors
and noble friends without whose support this book
would not exist.

Leading Sponsors
The Ottolino Family ~ Anna, Paul, Sara, Anthony, and Sam
Malek Abdel-Fattah

Additional Treasured Sponsors (in alphabetical order)
Lori and Kevin Braun
Marilyn Dyre
Nelson Insulation Company
Tod Nelson
Marylou P. Nunamaker
Nancy Schwab
Helen Trop-Zell

Gratitude

T HE STORY BEHIND a book often begins long before
the writing of the book, and *Sitting on the Toolbox*
is no exception. I want to begin by thanking my teachers
in Sri Lanka who filled me with Buddha's wisdom and
taught me what it means to be a monk.

Next I offer sincere appreciation for the many people
at Blue Lotus Temple and Meditation Center whose
emotional and logistical support, not to mention kindness and friendship, sustain me in countless ways. I
simply could not do what I do without you.

As for those who have most directly had a hand in
the physical creation of this book, thank you to Jessica
Dunegan for your care and artistry in designing such a
vibrant book cover. For interior design and layout, deep
thanks to Hynek Palatin for your expertise, precision,
generosity, and supreme professionalism. And warm
thanks to Amber Byers of Tadpole Press for proofreading
the final manuscript with good cheer and consideration.

I offer heartfelt gratitude to Stacey Stern for working with me so skillfully and joyfully to bring this book into the world. As a monk, it can be difficult to find someone who can engage in a wide range of deep spiritual discussions and who truly understands and appreciates the nuances. Stacey is among those rare people.

She has vast knowledge of Buddha's teachings, and she has reflected a great deal about her experiences of putting them into practice. Throughout our collaboration, Stacey quickly understood what I wanted to convey and was able to capture my voice and my experiences. One of the best things about Stacey is that she can deeply feel someone's heart. I believe that means her heart is pure, genuine, and practical.

Anna and Paul Ottolino deserve extra special acknowledgment. More than friends, they are family to me. Thank you, Anna and Paul, for your generous sponsorship of this book and so many of my endeavors.

Profound gratitude, as always, to Buddha.

And deep gratitude to you, dear reader and fellow traveler.

Note from the Authors

THIS BOOK IS A DREAM come true for us. We'll show you why through a quick trip to the past and back.

At the age of eleven, Bhante Sujatha was ordained as a Buddhist monk in his native Sri Lanka. After living the first twenty years of his life in the East, Bhante made his way West and founded the Blue Lotus Temple and Meditation Center in Woodstock, Illinois, in 2002.

A compassionate soul and gifted speaker, Bhante travels the world helping others by sharing Buddha's wisdom. To spread more joy and reach more people, Bhante looked for many years for the right writing partner to create this very book.

Meanwhile, back when Bhante was eleven and beginning his life as a Buddhist monk, Stacey, also eleven at the time, was being trained in meditation in her native Maryland. For the next forty years, Bhante and Stacey lived very different lives, traveling their own spiritual paths, until being introduced by their dear mutual friends Anna and Paul Ottolino.

It's been nothing short of magical since then.

From the start, it was evident that each was the person the other was seeking. Stacey had turned to Buddhist teachings and her own practice for insight and guidance throughout her adulthood, and while she often found comfort and clarity, that wasn't always the case. Occasionally, she had less than optimal results when applying to her life what she understood to be Buddhist wisdom. In Bhante, Stacey discovered a remarkable human being as well as a precious resource with whom to delve deeper into Buddha's teachings and their applications to contemporary life—for the benefit of others.

Stacey's desire was in perfect alignment with Bhante's calling to spread Buddha's wisdom more widely in the Western world through simple, clear language and from the distinct perspective of an Eastern man living in America. Although Bhante has been doing this tirelessly at Blue Lotus Temple and through extensive travels throughout the US and abroad, sitting down to focus on and write the book he long envisioned was another story.

As we sat down to write *Sitting on the Toolbox*, we promised each other that we would challenge one another creatively and intellectually every step of the way by discussing and questioning our personal experiences with Buddha's teachings. Bhante joked that our ongoing inquiry and exchange might even lead us to enlightenment. While neither of us would make that claim, we have loved learning and growing as we created this book for you.

So thank you, dear reader, for inspiring us. Even when you didn't realize we were thinking about you, we were, as we sought to write a book that would serve you well. We sincerely hope you are enriched by what you discover on these pages and within yourself. You already are providing benefit to others in that proceeds from book sales are being donated to three special causes.

The first is Bhante's Incubator Project, which purchases incubators that save the lives of prematurely born children in Sri Lanka. The second is Bhante's Pregnant Mothers Retreat. Every summer 300 pregnant women from throughout central Sri Lanka gather at Sri Subodharama International Buddhist Center for a three-day retreat during which Bhante guides the women in meditations for themselves and their babies. The expectant mothers are nurtured in mind, body, and community, before returning to their respective homes with care packages that support their continued well-being. The third is Bhante's newest project, which is to raise funds to purchase a much-needed ultrasound machine for the maternity ward at the Peradeniya General Hospital in Sri Lanka.

From this point onward, this book is written in Bhante's voice and imbued with love and blessings from both of us.

To your joy!

Venerable Bhante Sujatha and Stacey Stern

Introduction

You are sitting on the toolbox

EACH ONE OF US is born with spiritual tools that get obscured over time. Under the influence of even well-intentioned friends, families, teachers, and society as a whole, we often lose touch with our innate wisdom.

The great news is that even on our darkest days, deep spiritual truths lie within us, awaiting our mindful attention. In this way, we each sit upon our own toolbox—our own treasure trove of inner resources. I am honored to guide you back to yours.

This book is structured to parallel a seeker's journey. Part One, "Opening the Toolbox," establishes a relatable foundation about problems in everyday modern life and key elements in the spiritual journey. Part Two, "More Daily Tools," addresses challenges we contend with as we move through life—ego, fear, anger, and grief—and is filled with stories about how to lessen suffering. Part Three, "Drilling Deeper," delves into what makes life richer as we move beyond surviving and into thriving through forgiveness, loving-kindness, mindfulness, and joy.

If you read this book from start to finish, you will be guided on a progressive journey of exploration. However, each chapter can also stand on its own. If you are drawn to a particular topic, feel free to begin there. You will notice that the chapters vary in length. Some are short, while others are longer to convey aspects of those particular teachings. Each chapter also has its own distinct flavor. If one is not to your liking, please try another.

Buddha famously used storytelling to illuminate the human condition, and I enjoy doing the same. These pages are filled with a mix of modern and ancient tales. For the anecdotes from my own life or the lives of people I know, I've typically changed people's names and other identifying features to protect their privacy. Other stories have been passed down through centuries of oral and written Buddhist discourse.

Because many Buddhist teachings incorporate Pali or Sanskrit words, I have italicized those words the first time they are used. For those familiar with Buddhist teachings, you likely know the word *sutra*. Sutra is a Sanskrit word that literally means "string" or "thread." In the Indian literary traditions, sutra can refer to collections of teachings, statements, or rules.

In Sri Lanka we use the word *sutta* (the Pali language word for sutra) to describe the teachings of Guatama

Buddha, also known as Siddhartha Guatama, or simply, Buddha. He is believed to have lived mostly in the eastern part of ancient India around the fourth or fifth centuries BCE.

Suttas come from the Pali Canon, which contains the central teachings of Theravada Buddhism, the tradition in which I was raised. When I reference the names of people from the suttas and other words common in Theravada Buddhism, I often use their Pali spellings. Those accustomed to seeing the Sanskrit version of these words will notice some differences. Please check out the Glossary at the end of this book for a handy reference to some of the Buddhist terminology I use and my simple definitions.

As is often the case with oral tradition—especially when it derives from ancient languages that are interpreted and reinterpreted by many people over time—suttas can vary when told by one person to the next. Perhaps you previously have heard some of these suttas and they were not exactly as I tell them. That is okay.

Suttas are filled with wisdom, and the person delivering them may choose to emphasize certain aspects in service to specific teachings. As an Eastern man who spent the first half of my life in Asia and the second half (to date) in America, I alter aspects of suttas to make them more relatable to modern Western audiences.

If the ancient Buddhist stories on the pages that follow are completely new to you, welcome to these teachings! If you have heard variations of some of these before, I invite you to enjoy my versions and see if something new in you is sparked.

Whether you are a complete novice or well versed in Buddhism, I hope this book serves you. Each chapter concludes with an "Integrating Insight" section—three questions or action steps to help you incorporate Buddha's wisdom into your life. To ensure you have plenty of space to answer the questions, write down your reflections, and record your discoveries as you implement the action steps, you may want to keep a journal, tablet, or laptop nearby. If you own the book in your hands, feel free to mark up the pages with your notes and thoughts—this can be a cool way to track your evolving perspectives.

I also encourage you to discuss your "Integrating Insight" experiences with trusted family members and friends. By including them in your journey, you can receive support and increased accountability. In turn, as you grow in awareness and joy, they will benefit as well.

You may notice that the "Integrating Insight" section is designed for individual as well as group use. If you are in a book club or other study or social group, you can use the questions and action steps as prompts for group discussion and ongoing exploration.

As with everything in life, the more care and attention you give something, the more you will receive in return. Please enjoy, consider, integrate, and revisit these teachings to your heart and soul's content. Revel in the spiritual treasures you discover within yourself.

Ready to open your toolbox? I'll be right by your side.

Part One

OPENING THE TOOLBOX

It begins with increased awareness

1

Everybody Has Problems

LET'S BEGIN WITH something beautiful. A smile. I am smiling now as I think of you and your beautiful soul, and I invite you to smile with me. Perhaps you will accept my invitation and feel joy rise within you. Or maybe you won't. You're sad. You're tired. Life feels hard. You don't want to smile even if a monk invites you to smile. That's okay. It's up to you. If you don't feel like it now, maybe you will later.

People often ask, "Bhante, why are you always smiling? Is it because you are a monk? Because you have no problems?"

I have many problems. We all do. Problems are part of being human and being in a body. But even though we all face difficulties in our lives, we also can smile. When I see someone smile, I feel happy. Not because it means everything's necessarily fabulous in their life, but because it's a sign that Buddha exists in them.

Every time you smile, it is as if a tiny Buddha inside you is trying to come out. Let him come out. Don't push him down. In case this sounds odd, I will explain. My favorite ways to explain things are through stories and personal experiences.

As Founder and Spiritual Director of Blue Lotus Buddhist Temple and Meditation Center outside Chicago, I am honored that so many people share their concerns with me. It has taught me a great deal about the many ways Westerners suffer.

I recently had a conversation with someone I'll call John, who approached me after an evening service.

"Bhante, I am done with my job. I am sick and tired of it. There is no way I am going back to work tomorrow."

"I am sorry you're so unhappy, John. I understand. But for now, just go home, and please call me in the morning."

The next morning, John called me from his car while he was driving to work.

"You're on your way to work? Last night you told me you weren't going back. What happened?"

"Last night I was disappointed. I was angry, but I have to go to work."

"What time did you wake up? How has your morning been so far?"

"I got up at the crack of dawn because I have to be at the office at 8:45 a.m., and first I need to take my kids to school and drop my wife off at her job. I'm now stuck in traffic and will get to work late. My boss gets angry with me whenever I'm late, and the day usually goes downhill from there.

When I told you last night that I wasn't going back to work, I was tired and frustrated and just wanted to vent. But even as I told you that, I knew I'd go to work today. I have to. My family depends on me and my paycheck."

"Perhaps it's time to meet with your boss, John, to discuss how to improve things for both of you, or maybe it's time to start looking for a preferable job that also provides you with enough money to care for your family. You know you want to make changes, so make changes. In the meantime, try to appreciate whatever you can about your current situation—the financial security, your healthy family and the love you share, and whatever else comes to mind.

So today you woke up early, had a hectic morning, and are battling traffic. It's simply what you are doing today for the job you have right now. Why do it unhappily? Find a way to do it happily. If you want to make it better, you can. If you want to hold onto discomfort and misery, you can. Either way, it's your choice."

* * *

Whether or not you relate to John's frustrations, life is full of unpleasant situations. Often it's only when we flip the negatives to their opposite that we can see something beautiful. Perhaps you're thinking, "Life's not that simple," or "My problems are much bigger than John's," or "That's just magical thinking. It won't change anything."

What I offer throughout this book is not about "positive thinking" or pretending to feel differently than you do. It is about seeing through what you think is the whole story to the possibilities inside and allowing that to shift your experience.

I intentionally began with a simple, common situation. Many people are unhappy with their jobs, their routines, and their daily responsibilities. I address this and much, much more in the pages ahead. Most importantly, I show you how you can have a more joyful life no matter your external circumstances.

In Buddhist teachings, there is a story of a clay pot that I like to tell like this. A clay pot sits on a table with a glowing candle inside that can't be seen from the outside. The clay pot is thick and heavy, completely obscuring the light within.

As you approach the table, you take a closer look at the pot. You notice it has a lid. Curious, you remove the lid and peek inside. That's when you first glimpse the glowing candle. After you put the lid back on, someone else walks into the room.

"There's a candle burning brightly inside this pot," you say.

"Impossible," they say. "I would see some evidence, some light coming out from it. I see nothing but a dark pot."

You want to show this person the light, but now the lid won't open. You try again to lift the lid. It is stuck. It won't budge. You know there is a candle inside and you want to let the light out. What can you do? The only way to let the light out now is to break the pot, but you are scared to do that.

Often we think the clay pot is what's valuable and that it's more important to keep the pot whole than to let the light out. But one dark day, you decide the light is more precious than the pot. You break the pot and light floods the room.

Remember that tiny Buddha inside you that I mentioned before? Often this is referred to as *Buddha-nature*, the possibility to be content. More than that, it is the ability to build upon our basic goodness and evolve.

From the moment we are born into this world, we carry a bright light deep inside. As babies and young children, others bask in our light. As we grow, we pick up worries, concerns, and negativities that form a thick layer around our inner light. You may think these accumulated beliefs make you who you are and define you. They don't. They aren't the real you. The real you is the candle inside. You are luminous.

In precious moments, we catch glimpses of our true nature—our Buddha-nature. Usually this happens when we temporarily unhook from the distractions of daily life, such as when we are out in nature, when we are still, or when we see our basic goodness reflected back through the eyes of a loved one.

I see a hint of Buddha-nature in every smile. Whether or not you see it or feel it yet, trust me. Your lightness comes out when you genuinely smile. Each one of us can share our beautiful nature in many ways and invite others to do the same. When we do, we don't simply fill a room with light like the candle in the clay pot. We fill the entire world with light and love.

Integrating Insight

1. What is the number one problem troubling you right now?

2. Did you read anything in this chapter that offered a new perspective on the problem? If so, what was it? If not, perhaps you can take another look at the chapter, with your specific problem in mind. As you read, feel free to underline or highlight anything you feel encouraged by.

3. Even if you aren't yet aware of the light you release when you smile, start to pay attention to whether or not you can see it in the smiles of others.

2

Wounded Minds

THE GREAT NEWS is we all have Buddha-nature inside. The not-so-great news is we also have wounded minds. No one is immune. Whether your childhood was terrible, wonderful, or both, you have experienced pain, disappointment, fear, anger, sadness, and loss. The cumulative emotional damage we suffer as human beings is what I refer to as "wounded mind."

When we understand that everyone has a wounded mind, we are more compassionate and can begin to heal our minds and ourselves. The healthier we are, the better we can help others. One way to facilitate healing a wounded mind is through a simple loving-kindness meditation or practice. When I was teaching this many years ago, a student named Anne gave me a powerful lesson about the depth of wounds.

I had been meeting regularly in Illinois with a small group of men and women who were interested in meditation instruction. One day, without advance notice,

I decided to change the technique and announced that we were going to do a loving-kindness meditation for the first time.

Everyone seemed game. "Sure! Let's do it!" (By the way, enthusiasm to try something new is one of the many things I love about Americans.) I asked everyone to find a comfortable sitting position, close their eyes, and take a few deep breaths. Then I invited them to repeat after me, "I am well. I am happy. I am peaceful." Together, we repeated these three sentences aloud several more times, until the words began to settle in.

I began the next round with, "May my brothers, sisters, parents, children, neighbors, coworkers, and friends be well, be happy, be peaceful." We continued with that for a little while before moving on to the final round, "May all beings everywhere be well, be happy, be peaceful." We repeated that for a bit, then sat in silence together.

Anne was seated directly in front of me. She regularly attended my meditation classes. She always seemed happy and often joked with me. Since I am a joker, we had a nice rapport.

When I asked the group, "How do you like loving-kindness meditation?" Anne was the first to reply. She immediately declared, "I hate loving-kindness meditation."

At first I thought she was joking, so I laughed, but then I realized she was quite upset. I had never seen that side of her before.

"Why do you hate loving-kindness meditation?"

"Because the first part is so selfish. I can practice loving-kindness for other people. No problem. I do it all the time. If I direct it toward myself, it is not right. It is selfish."

When Anne said that, I realized I had more to learn about American culture. I never heard someone from Sri Lanka say that loving-kindness meditation is selfish. Anne helped me understand her perspective, which is one shared by many Westerners.

Anne continued, "According to my Christian up-bringing, I was taught not to think about myself, but instead to think about others."

"If you aren't loving toward yourself, how can you be loving toward other people?"

"That's easy. I do it every day. I've been involved with the homeless program at the church for fifteen years. I am loving and kind to all the homeless people."

Even though Anne seemed convinced she was able to be genuinely and completely loving to others without loving herself, I sensed that something was off and thought I might be able to get to it if I changed the topic.

"Okay, my friend. Let me ask you to imagine this. Christmas is coming, and you decide you want to give me a gift. Giving gifts is a big deal in this country. It's not in my country. But here, not only is it a big part of your culture, there also are certain expectations around it.

For example, when you give me a gift, I am supposed to open it right away. In my country, no way. If somebody gives a gift in Sri Lanka, we don't open it in front of them. To do so might offend the giver. We wait until that person leaves, and we open it in private.

But we are in America, and now we're pretending that you plan to give me a gift. You select it carefully, wrap it nicely, and are very excited to give it to me. After I receive your gift, I am supposed to say something like, 'Thank you! This is the best gift I have ever received. I never before received such a gift in my whole life. You are the only one to ever give me this kind of gift.'

Why am I supposed to say all those words? To make you happy. Those words are not for my benefit. Now, imagine instead that you hand me your gift and I set it aside because I'm talking to somebody. I don't acknowledge in that moment that you just gave me a lovely gift. How would that make you feel?"

"Insulted."

"Yes, and perhaps angry and disappointed. Maybe you'd be thinking, 'I can't believe this monk doesn't know how to say thank you.'"

There were some chuckles in the room. Anne looked annoyed. Even so, I was quite surprised when she blurted out, "You are a terrible Buddhist monk!"

A hush fell across the room. I took a deep breath and replied, "I can handle that. Yes, I can handle that. I have just one more question for you. In the story I just made up, when you gave me the gift, did you think you were practicing loving-kindness toward me?"

"Yes. That's why I spent my money."

"No. That's not why you spent your money. You spent your money so I would appreciate you more. That is selfish. If you give me a gift, you must give it fully, without holding onto it in your mind, ego, or anywhere. Once you give me a gift, it is mine to hold, and I may do whatever I want with it. But in this story, even though you physically gave me the gift, you were still clinging to it mentally.

After I received your gift, I should thank you and express my appreciation. That is my job, my responsibility. If I don't do that, then I should address that. However, if you expect me to open your gift in front of you and express my appreciation on the spot in a certain way, that expectation is your problem. That's what I meant before when I said you were selfish. You weren't fully giving me the gift. You were still holding onto it, or at least holding onto your expectations of how I should receive it."

Anne did not like this explanation. Nor was she pleased that a few more people in the room were now giggling. Grabbing her purse, she said, "I don't like you.

You hurt my feelings. You are not a good Buddhist monk. These people are laughing at me. I'm leaving." Then she stormed out.

What could I do? Nothing. I couldn't force her to stay. She did what she needed to do for herself in the moment. All eyes were on me as the other students watched to see how I would react. I didn't do anything except smile and say to the group, "Calm down. It's okay." Then we continued our lesson.

That is not the end of the story though. Anne went home and continued to stew over what had happened. That night she wrote me a very long email berating me for what I said to her in class.

I responded with an email expressing my concern for her. Here is part of what I wrote, "My dear friend, I care about you. I know you believe you are angry with me, but I don't think that is the whole truth. I am concerned that you actually hate yourself. This is one reason why you were so uncomfortable with the part of the loving-kindness meditation that was about being loving and kind to yourself. I was trying to show you that weakness and am sorry I wasn't able to help you see that. I hope you can figure out how to heal your wounded mind."

Anne sent me another angry email in response. Among other things, she wrote, "I don't like your teaching. I don't like loving-kindness. You are a fake Buddhist monk."

A fake Buddhist monk? Never had I been accused of that. It was a bit of a shock, and it stung. I had to accept that Anne viewed me that way. "Okay, it's fine," I told myself. "If Anne sees me as phony, that's how she sees me."

I sent another caring email and received another bitter response. Now she was pushing my buttons. My loving-kindness is not my foolishness. Nor should yours be. I write much more about this in the "Loving-Kindness" section of this book.

I decided I'd had enough, and I wrote something like this to Anne, "Here's the deal. This is the last email I will send you. You can send me as many emails as you want, but I will not reply. In fact, I will not even open or read them. I will immediately delete them."

Anne continued to send me emails, and I deleted them as they came in. This continued for several months.

One day I received an email from her with the subject line, "Be kind to me. Please read." I thought, "No problem. I am ready to read this now."

When I opened her email and started reading, I began to cry. Her story went something like this:

"Bhante, today is my fortieth birthday. When I was ten years old, I lived in Los Angeles with my mother, who was a drug addict and alcoholic. She abused me physically, mentally, and emotionally. I hate her and no longer have any connection with her. I came to the Chicago area when I was a teenager.

As I walked by the Unitarian Universalist church one day and saw a small sign outside for the Blue Lotus Meditation Group, I thought it might be a nice place for me to relax. That's why I joined your meditation group."

(I want to pause here a moment to note that people come to meditation for many different reasons. Anne simply wanted to relax. She didn't want to learn anything deep or profound. I write more about meditation in the next chapter, but for now, I'll return to Anne's story.)

"You were so joyful, so funny. We laughed together. I had a lot of fun at the group until, out of the middle of nowhere, you began talking about self-healing and self-love, which I really didn't like.

As I continued to reflect on why I was so resistant to it, I realized it was because if I became kind and loving to everyone, I couldn't hate my mother anymore. I wasn't ready to stop hating her. I argued with you because you were saying things I didn't want to hear. I have really been struggling with this.

But today, on my fortieth birthday, I decided enough was enough. I was so tired of the struggle, and I was finally ready to let it go. I prayed, 'I want to surrender! I want to let this go!'

Immediately I felt tremendous relief and so much love for myself. I also felt so much love for my mother. Can you believe that? So much love for my mother.

I suddenly understood that if my mother knew better, she would have treated me better. She was a single mother, and I am grateful to her. She raised me without breaking my legs and arms. She raised me, and I am grateful for that."

I was deeply touched by what Anne wrote and proud of the hard work she was doing to heal. I responded, "You got it! Now continue your journey." I didn't specifically invite her back to the Blue Lotus Meditation Group. The group is open, and I figured if she wants to come back, she will.

Time passed. Anne didn't return.

Months later, as I prepared for class on a cold winter morning, an elderly woman entered the room through the disability access door. I had never seen her before. She was moving slowly with her walker. As I approached her to offer my assistance, I saw that someone was coming in right behind her. I guessed it was her daughter. "How sweet," I thought. "A woman is bringing her mother to meditation practice."

It was Anne! The daughter was Anne! I was shocked. Anne had decided to return to the meditation group with her mother.

Anne's mother ending up coming to my meditation classes for three years before she passed away. I called her "Grandmother," and she always made sure I ate well. We had a great time together.

Anne became very involved at the temple. I'd often say to her, "You are a saint," and I meant it from the bottom of my heart. Anne didn't complain or harbor anger. She was consistently generous, kind, and loving. She was able to show up this way for others because she had started with herself. She healed her own wounded mind. Although Anne did the hard work of healing herself, she'd say to me, "Bhante, what you did for my life, you must continue doing for others. I will help you however I can."

I have met countless people who suffer deeply from a wounded mind. Many are very good at hiding it from others. To each one of them—and to you—I say, "Please try loving-kindness. With regular practice, it can work wonders."

Start with yourself. Use these three phrases in the beginning.

I am well.
I am happy.
I am peaceful.

Say them as often as you like. Set aside at least a few minutes every day for a focused loving-kindness meditation. Continue to repeat these phrases silently throughout the day and evening. You can do this while in the car at red lights and stop signs, when standing in line, or in between activities.

Any time is a good time for loving-kindness.

Integrating Insight

1. Can you recognize your own wounded mind? If so, what are some particularly ingrained wounds or negative mindsets?

2. If you can't, see if you can begin to notice your own patterns of reactivity. Are there certain people or situations that make you particularly uncomfortable?

3. If you don't already have a regular loving-kindness practice, consider setting aside five minutes a day to say silently or aloud, "I am well. I am happy. I am peaceful."

3

Key Elements in the Spiritual Journey

EACH OF US IS A SPIRIT living inside a body. When we come into the world as babies, we are filled with divine nature. Yet being born in a body also requires that we contend with animal nature—the basic drives and needs that all animals have.

As we grow up in a distracted world, it can be easy to heed the pull of our animal instincts and feel as if we are drifting away from our divine nature, our inherent spirituality. But that is an illusion. Our divine nature—our Buddha-nature—is always within us. Sometimes it is obscured like the light in the clay pot, but it is always part of us.

Reconnecting with our inner light and wisdom is what the spiritual journey is about. We do this when we pay attention to our minds and actions, cultivate the good, and surround ourselves with people who also are committed to this.

I define the three key elements in the spiritual journey as noble friendship, mindful observation, and cultivating the mind. I'll walk you through them with a mix of ancient and modern stories.

1. Noble Friendship

The Ghatikara Sutta tells of a legendary friendship between two men, Ghatikara and Jotipala. Ghatikara was a potter from a low caste who was a devoted follower of the Buddha of his time, Kassapa Buddha.

Ghatikara repeatedly invited his dear friend to come listen to Buddha with him. But each time, Jotipala refused, saying something like, "Spirituality is not my thing."

This troubled Ghatikara because he strongly believed that it was important for his friend to receive Buddha's teachings. He was convinced that if Jotipala came with him to the temple just once, he would be transformed simply by being in Buddha's presence.

Ghatikara became increasingly determined that his friend come and see Buddha for himself. "Isn't this what friends are for?" he thought. With this in mind, he asked yet again. This time when Jotipala refused, Ghatikara grabbed him by the hair and pleaded with him.

Although Jotipala was shocked by Ghatikara's forceful approach, he reasoned that Ghatikara must be under some kind of a spell from Buddha to behave as he did.

"If my meeting Buddha is really so important to you, I'll go. I have no interest in Buddha, as you know, but I will do this for you because you are my friend."

When they arrived at the temple, Ghatikara went directly to the front row so he could listen intently to Buddha, while Jotipala seated himself in the back of the room. He didn't want to be there, but since he was, he might as well listen to what Buddha had to say.

To his great surprise, Jotipala was deeply affected by Buddha's words. So much so that he approached Buddha immediately afterward and asked if he would accept him as his student.

Buddha honored his wish and conferred the higher ordination on him. Jotipala entered the Noble Order the next day. Ghatikara could not join his friend in his pursuit of a higher state of being because he needed to continue to care for his blind parents. Yet their friendship continued in remarkable ways throughout that lifetime and beyond.

As Jotipala was nearing the end of his life, he entered a place outside of ordinary time and space and later returned to earth as Siddhartha Guatama—he reincarnated as Buddha!

Jotipala had no idea this was his fate when his dear friend Ghatikara begged him to go to the temple. In fact, he probably thought Ghatikara was being a pain in the butt. That's often what I have thought about the noble friends who have pushed me to learn, think, and grow beyond my own comfort zone. Of course I say that with a smile because what I mostly feel is deep love and gratitude for all the wonderful teachers who have guided me.

Yet there is more to this story. Many years later when Guatama Buddha was asked if half of a holy life is about good and noble friends, he replied that it wasn't half. Rather, noble friendship is, "The *whole* of this holy life, this friendship, companionship, and association with the good."

2. Mindful Observation

The second key element in a spiritual journey is mindful observation. If you want to become more aware of yourself and others and make better choices, you must sit quietly and observe your own mind.

The first thing you'll likely notice when you try to observe your mind is that your thoughts don't stay in one place. They move around. They wander. So many thoughts, feelings, and emotions will arise. We call this monkey mind. Watch and befriend your own monkey mind.

Those who have tried to make peace with their monkey mind may say, "Easier said than done." Agreed. It does take practice. Lots of practice.

Yet the alternative looks something like this: Your days are filled with reacting to whatever happens in your body and mind. Your reactions are based on whether you identify the thoughts and feelings as good or bad, as things you like or dislike. You continually feed these cycles of reactivity. Life feels like a roller coaster, always going up or down in accordance with your likes and dislikes. Very rarely can you rest in a neutral space. You don't experience sustained periods of calm, clarity, or peace.

However, once you begin to observe your mind—without immediately reacting to or judging it—you will see that you are choosing the roller coaster. You are allowing yourself to constantly bounce back and forth between your likes and dislikes, your desires and fears.

This perspective can help you get off the roller coaster if you want. It can lead to balance, equanimity, and a place where you can learn to observe yourself and your life with a sense of neutrality. If something positive happens, you observe that something positive happened. If something negative happens, you observe that something negative happened. You will come to understand that what we label as positive and what we label as negative are always changing.

You will also see that the stories you tell yourself about your life are your own creations. They are not necessarily real. You are the one who gives your stories energy and continues to feed them.

The more you observe your mind, the more you will be able to discern reality from illusion. Difficult feelings will loosen their grip. Since everything is always changing, and our minds cloud reality with stories, why act from a place of distress or reaction? When you are able to observe what happens in your mind and body without making judgments, discomfort can pass. You can let angst go. This is what is possible with mindful observation.

If someone studies and even memorizes all of Buddha's teachings (known as *dharma* in Sanskrit or *dhamma* in Pali), what is the value? I know people who have so much collective information about the dharma, but they don't know how to put it into practice. They read, read, read, then read some more. They are walking libraries.

But if they don't put what they read into practice, they are in trouble. The first step to putting teachings into practice is to observe your mind. You can read all about loving-kindness, for example, but how can you behave lovingly if you have lots of latent anger inside?

It's natural to push down and repress uncomfortable feelings like anger, pain, fear, and shame. Sometimes our survival depends on it. But surviving and thriving are two very different things.

If you want to live a happier, more fulfilling life, you must learn to observe your own mind. I assure you that you will find lots of anger, hurt, and pain inside. That's when you can begin to work with these emotions.

The reason we are here on earth is to learn how to be more loving. To love others well, we first must learn how to love ourselves. Observing your mind is one of the most loving things you can do.

You can even use love and compassion to heal the wounds you discover inside your own mind. That's what I do. When I notice I'm having a steady stream of anxious thoughts, the first thing I say to those thoughts is, "I love you."

This is the opposite of what we might want to say to those troubling feelings. Our first instinct might be to generate more anger or frustration. Perhaps we hate those awful thoughts and hate ourselves for thinking them. But when you put another negative emotion on top of what already feels bad, you create more pain. You dig yourself into a deeper hole.

If you want to overcome anxieties, you must befriend your concerns. Gently ask yourself, "Why am I so sad right now? Why am I worried in this moment?"

When you remain quiet, answers will emerge. You will begin to get clearer. Then you can ask more questions and learn more. The more you learn, the better able you are to address each problem at its root.

Sometimes there will be specific actions you can take to resolve a bothersome situation. In other cases, you may recognize that you are allowing yourself to be haunted by an old hurt that no longer has a purpose.

Since you don't need to hold onto it to keep you safe, you can compassionately let it go.

3. Cultivating the Mind

Many Westerners turn to meditation as a way to relax, but I view meditation's most important function as helping us cultivate our minds. This is an active practice, not a relaxing one.

Bhavana is the word we use for meditation in both Pali and Sanskrit. It literally means developing, cultivating, or producing, in the sense of calling into existence. It often is paired with another word to describe what is being cultivated. For example, *metta-bhavana* refers to the development or cultivation of loving-kindness. When used on its own, bhavana signifies contemplation or mental and spiritual cultivation.

While this kind of mental training requires discipline and focus, the rewards are tremendous. I will get to the rewards a little later in this chapter, providing you right now with an opportunity for delayed gratification.

Seriously though, I have met countless people who struggle with meditation. Shortly after I arrived in the United States in the 1990s, a man came up to me after a talk I gave and said, "Bhante, I have been practicing meditation for fifteen years. Fifteen years!"

"How wonderful," I said.

His response surprised me. "It's not wonderful at all. I am so confused. I have taken meditation classes with so many teachers, and they all give different instructions. 'Breathe from your belly.' 'Breathe through your nose.' 'Don't pay attention to your breath at all. Ignore your breath. Instead, focus on your thoughts and label them.' 'No, don't focus on your thoughts, just let them go.' I am frustrated and miserable. You are a monk. What is the right way to meditate?"

As I listened to this man asking whether he should breathe from his nose or his belly, I considered that the answers to those questions might not even be found in Buddha's teachings. Buddha didn't get into the kind of details that Westerners seem to like.

In Sri Lanka monks are the primary meditation teachers, and their instructions are fairly straightforward. They tell us to begin by breathing in and out naturally to help settle the body and mind. With a calm breath, we can have a calm life.

Only when we are calm can we penetrate what is happening inside us. Energy is like a pond. When the water is stirred up and murky, we can't see what lies beneath the surface. Similarly, fast breathing and distracted thoughts prevent us from seeing our own inner depths.

This is why we are instructed to focus on our in-breath and our out-breath to prepare for meditation. This helps us settle ourselves so we can observe what lies inside us as it truly is. Then we look closely at our minds, paying attention to exactly what is happening. This is how we identify and untangle the roots of our problems.

For example, you might discover that the root of one particular thing you're angry about lies in your expectations about that situation. Expectations that perhaps you created or built up, and that now are causing you pain. When you see this clearly, you can begin to cut out the roots. If you so choose, you can release your expectations and the anger they have been fueling.

The more you observe your mind, the better you will know yourself. You will see where the many roots of suffering arise from, how they are interconnected, and how you feed them. You also will notice the ways in which you push your angst onto others, especially your loved ones, and cause them to suffer as well. Then you can decide if you are ready to cut out the roots of your pain and begin to heal.

* * *

A week or so after the man who had been unhappily meditating for fifteen years told me about his confusion, I better understood his feelings of overwhelm when I was asked to do a simple errand. Driving home from an evening meditation class I taught, one of my brother monks (a fellow monk and housemate of mine) called to say we were running out of tea at home, and he asked me to please pick some up at the store.

No problem. I come from the Ceylon region where tea is grown. I know about tea, or at least I thought I did. Being new to the US, this was one of the first times I had ventured into a massive American grocery store.

When I asked an employee where I could find tea, he led me to a long aisle with thousands of boxes of tea. I could hardly believe my eyes. There were so many to choose from. I had no idea what my brother monk wanted.

When I called and asked him what kind of tea he wanted, he was confused by my question. "What are you talking about? I just want tea."

So I began picking up the packages and reading the labels to learn more. One kind of tea was for sleep. One was for hiccups. One was for stress. One was to stay alert. One was called Pregnancy Tea. I knew we didn't need that one. The one called Yogi's tea said it would calm the mind and bring inner peace and tranquility. So many promises on a box of tea!

I became flustered about which tea to buy. Can all these tea boxes be true? I noticed I was definitely not feeling calm or peaceful in that moment. As I paused in the tea aisle to observe my mind and body, I was aware that I was tired from a long day of teaching and that I was getting sucked into tea box promises.

With this awareness, I could break the spell. I understood I wasn't stressed because this was actually an important decision, but rather because I had temporarily gotten stuck in a "weak mind moment." When we are experiencing weakness of the mind or emotions, it is easy to believe we need whatever someone is trying to sell us. This happens to even the smartest of people. Observing our mind and being clear about our needs and values can help us avoid this trap.

I also offer this story as an example of what it looks like to practice mindfulness in the midst of everyday life. Observing and cultivating your mind isn't just for when you're quiet and doing your sitting practice. We sit on the cushion or chair so that we can bring greater awareness of ourselves into all our interactions in the world.

There is always more to learn about ourselves and how we feel about new and different situations. I had been meditating for more than twenty years by the time I stood in that tea aisle in a grocery store outside Chicago—and still I experienced a weak mind moment. I always am grateful for the opportunity to observe and cultivate my mind.

So let's return to the dilemma of the miserable meditator—the man who was frustrated after receiving fifteen years of meditation instruction from many different teachers. His feelings are understandable. Here in the

US, monks teach meditation, nuns teach meditation, and so do yogis, swamis, and gurus. It's as if all of India is here.

With the variety of spiritual teachers and practices offered, there is no shortage of options. While this is beneficial for many reasons, having a lot of opportunities and choices can also make you feel heavy.

It's natural to be curious and want to do some shopping at first. Meditation shopping, that is. Try classes with different teachers for a bit if you want to explore different techniques, but then just settle down and get to the work of meditating.

At its core, meditation is not about techniques. People love techniques. Sometimes, though, it's the moment that someone gives up the techniques that they begin meditating.

Meditating is about sitting down and looking within. Whether you focus on your breath or on labeling your thoughts or on a mantra isn't so important. Watching and observing yourself is what matters. Until you do that, whatever you learn, listen to, or read can take you only so far.

When you are looking for answers or teachers outside of yourself, you are not meditating. You must look within. Recognize and understand *your* difficulties so you can address them.

When we cultivate our minds, there is so much good we can do. Ask yourself what you want to cultivate in your mind and your life. Patience? Love? Kindness? Compassion? Forgiveness? Generosity? You may have a long list. Turn your attention inward to cultivate what you most desire in yourself and for the world.

Often I am asked, "Bhante, how do I know if I'm doing it right? How do I know if my meditation practice is working?"

Here is the answer. If your meditation practice is working, these four things will happen.

1. **You become so loving to yourself and others.**

   Loving yourself must come first. This means taking excellent care of your body and your mind. Only when you do this, can you love others without need or expectation.

2. **You become very compassionate.**

   This means you are able to feel other people's pains, challenges, and difficulties without hurting yourself. If you take on other people's pain so much that you hurt yourself, you can't be of service to them. Plus, you will have doubled the pain. They will still have their pain, and you will be carrying it too.

3. **You experience more joy.**
   You are genuinely happy for other people and rarely are jealous.

4. **You feel balanced because of equanimity.**
   Equanimity is what happens once you exit the daily emotional roller coaster of feeling happy one minute, unhappy the next. If something good happens, you accept it and enjoy it. If something bad happens, you accept it and simply be with it, knowing it too shall pass.

If your practice is going well, you will experience these four things. Allow that to give you confidence. Then continue working toward even higher states of mindfulness and awareness.

Meditation has two aspects. One is the sitting and the second is the applying it in real life. That's where the rubber meets the road, where it really counts. As Buddha taught in the Parahada Sutta, "Gradually train, gradually practice, gradually progress."

Integrating Insight

1. Who are your noble friends?

2. To whom are you a noble friend?

3. What takeaways from this chapter will you apply to establish or enhance your meditation practice?

4

Seeing Beauty

I WAS HAVING LUNCH with my students in a busy restaurant one spring day. As my dining companions talked amongst themselves, my eyes scanned the room. I love people-watching, and there was much to observe during the lunchtime rush that day. Whenever I am around others, I pay attention to my thoughts and feelings about what I see and hear. This is one of the ways I practice mindfulness.

A young family at a nearby table caught my eye. There was a mother, father, and their daughter who was about three years old. I watched the mother give the little girl paper and crayons so she could color while they waited for their food.

Although I couldn't see what she was drawing, I guessed it was a butterfly when she glanced down at her picture, then up at her mother and said, "Mommy, I love butterflies!" When her mother asked her why she loved butterflies, the young girl answered, "They are so beautiful. They can fly. I want to fly like a butterfly."

As I heard the little girl declare her love for butterflies, I thought, "How beautiful. How innocent. This is how this three-year-old girl is experiencing life in this moment. She delights in the beauty of butterflies. How many adults would say, 'I want to fly like a butterfly'? I've never heard a grown-up say that. By the time we reach adulthood, many of us are jaded. We often are stressed and distracted. But this little girl believes anything is possible." It warmed my heart to watch her joy.

Sitting at a table near that family was a group of teenagers who appeared to be eighteen or nineteen years old. They were texting on their cell phones and teasing one another. They became increasingly loud, and a couple of them started making fun of one of the girls at their table. They kept at it until she blurted out, "I hate my life!"

I could feel her anger. I took some deep breaths. In and out. In and out. What had I just witnessed over the course of a few minutes? An unhappy young woman who hates her life is sitting just a few feet away from a little girl who is overjoyed by the beauty of butterflies.

Anyone who has spent time with teenagers knows they have big ups and downs. Their moods can change in an instant. Yet in this moment, it seemed as if the young woman wasn't seeing anything positive in her life.

Even though that can be common behavior for teenagers, I found myself wondering, "Has she had many opportunities to experience love and beauty? Are there adults in her life who can guide her to find peace, comfort her when she's feeling sad, and help her work through what's difficult so she can envision positive outcomes?"

We all need this. While teenagers may express themselves more dramatically than adults, I don't know any adult who has not experienced their fair share (and more) of pain. We have been betrayed. We become disillusioned. We may have money troubles, health problems, or struggle with addiction. There are times when life can feel more negative than positive.

But even when we can't see or fully feel it, we are surrounded by beauty. It might be in the words of a stranger, an unexpected act of kindness, a child's laugh, or the glowing sky at sunset. We may be too hurt or preoccupied to notice. We don't look up at the sky or fully receive a compliment.

When you aren't seeing or feeling beauty, what can you do?

1. Begin Within

Beauty is always here. It's just that some people don't know where or how to look for it, or they don't take the time to find it. To see the beauty of this world, we must first see the beauty of our own mind. Beauty begins on the inside.

If your inside is dark and your mind feels murky like disturbed waters in a pond, you have some work to do. It's the work of mindful observation and cultivating the mind, which I described in the last chapter.

But seeing beauty doesn't require that you spend hours upon hours each week sitting on the cushion. You can simply pause for a few minutes each day to take a few deep breaths, relax, and look at what's happening inside you. This is the beginning of seeing beauty.

When life is going well and you're not overly busy, pausing for a brief meditation like this once or a few times a day might be fun and easy. However, it is when life is hectic and we are stressed that we most need to pause. If someone tells me they can't find even two minutes in a day to pause, I tell them to find ten. When we least want to pause is often when we need it the most.

Some people complain about the demands on their time and the logistical difficulties of fitting in meditation. To the person who says, "I know meditating is important and I feel better when I do it, but I just can't find the time right now," I ask, "Do you eat? Do you shower? Do you brush your teeth?"

We prioritize what matters to us. This includes that upon which our survival depends, as well as the activities that significantly enhance our time here on Earth. For me, meditation is both.

Some people avoid meditation because they don't want to be still with their thoughts or fears. Like Sue, whose five-year-old daughter, Kathy, was diagnosed with leukemia. Sue was devastated. At first when she sat still to quiet her mind, she imagined every worst-case scenario. I told Sue that was fear talking, and she didn't have to let it trap her.

I explained that the more she worried about Kathy, the less able she was to be a calm source of comfort for her. Since Sue was making herself sick with worry and exhaustion, how could she provide relaxed, loving energy to her daughter? I told Sue she had to take better care of herself if she wanted to show up for Kathy in the ways that Kathy most needed.

This isn't easy. One of the worst things a parent can experience is the suffering or serious illness of their child. It can feel completely consuming. Sue and I discussed this.

"Even though I know it would be better for Kathy if I could feel calmer, I just can't. I am worried all the time. Yesterday when I sat down for a few moments, all I saw were scary thoughts. I was breathing quickly and didn't feel any peace."

"Your breath is your life. When you are so distressed that your breath is fast and shallow, you won't be able to feel peace. It may be difficult, but please try again today.

This time you can remind yourself that as you take a few minutes to watch your breath—and as you invite it to settle—you are giving value to your life.

This is how you invite your life to calm down, even if for just a few moments. As you take care of your breath, you take care of your life. When you respect and value your breath and your life, you also show respect for other people's breaths and lives.

Your constant fretting isn't helping Kathy. The best way to care for her is to care for yourself, beginning with your breath. When you are quiet and calm, you can be more present for Kathy. You likely will notice small moments of beauty that arrive in the care she receives from doctors and nurses, or in the relief she experiences when she feels comfortable, or even in the perfectly ripe and juicy peach you share at breakfast."

Buddha said it best in the Samyutta Nikaya, "When watching after yourself, you watch after others. When watching after others, you watch after yourself."

2. Look Around
We live in a big world. I have met many Americans who have no idea what life is like for people in other countries, especially in much poorer ones. They don't realize how difficult every day can be when your most basic needs for food, water, and shelter are not met.

When surrounded by abundance, it can be easy to take so much for granted. Yet when we truly open our eyes to the material comforts in our lives, especially when we understand what others must do merely to survive each day, we can better appreciate the gifts and beauty all around us.

Not everything is beautiful of course. Even in this country with so much wealth, there are many, many people who aren't as fortunate as you. There may be families in your own communities, or not far beyond, who struggle to feed their children. It's up to each one of us to look for what may be hidden.

It's not hard to discover if you make an effort. For example, you may be surprised to learn how many children in nearby schools rely on a free or reduced fee school lunch. When you drive around, do you see people sleeping under bridges? There is no need to travel to a developing country to discover homelessness. Read the newspaper. Learn more about the challenges in your community, especially the ones that don't typically affect your life.

Then begin doing little things. Perhaps you give a homeless person an extra coat you no longer need. If someone in front of you in line at the market is struggling to come up with the cash to purchase their groceries, you can offer to pay their bill. You don't need to make any big plans in advance to do these random acts of loving-kindness. Just give in the moment when you see it is needed, and as it feels good and right to you.

Encourage this in your children as well. Let them know that others don't always have enough to eat. Suggest that if they notice this at school, they can share their lunch. Perhaps you send them to school with an extra lunch. Your son or daughter can be encouraged to offer it casually to a classmate, saying something like, "Oh, I brought a lunch for you today. This is for you." No big deal. Nothing to discuss.

The more we look around, the more we will notice people, places, and animals that can benefit from our loving-kindness. It's a gift that keeps on giving. Research shows that when you practice innocent compassion, your immune system gets a boost.

As you focus on being good to others, pay attention to those you serve. This will take your mind off your own worries and deepen your appreciation for all you have. Most people who do volunteer work discover strength in others and themselves. That's what I call seeing beauty.

3. Remember Impermanence
We all know the expressions "nothing lasts forever" and "the only constant is change," but most of us don't fully appreciate what they mean. For me, impermanence is beautiful.

Many of us find it scary or depressing to consider that so much in our lives will change and people we love will die, but I find it to be one of the most powerful concepts. I'm not saying it is a happy experience to lose something or someone we love. Of course not.

What I am saying is that regularly reflecting on the impermanent nature of all things and beings strengthens our appreciation of everything and everyone. If we perceive a particular experience or situation as negative, we may find comfort in knowing it will pass.

As for the people, places, and things we love, we typically fear they will change. They will. While it's natural to fear losing friends or lovers or family members, I don't consider this kind of fear to be a problem.

The fear of losing someone we love can be a good thing to experience. Perhaps you're thinking, "How can this fear be good? It's making me miserable."

Well, that's sort of my point. You get to choose. Do you want the fear that someday your beloved grandmother will die to make you miserable, or do you want to treasure her final weeks with as much happiness and connection as possible?

Of course this doesn't just apply to people who are ill, old, or whose end appears to be near. This applies to everyone. There are no guarantees about tomorrow. We only have today. We only have this moment.

We can choose to view fear as an opportunity to be fearless. When we're aware we're afraid of losing someone we love, we can love them more while they are here. As Buddha said in the Dhammapada, "All conditioned things are impermanent—when one sees this with wisdom, one turns away from suffering."

What about the teenager I mentioned at the beginning of this chapter who declared to her friends at lunch, "I hate my life"? If I paraphrased Buddha's quote above and said to her something like, "This too shall pass . . . these difficult teen years will pass . . . everything is impermanent . . . know this and do not suffer," I am not sure she would believe me.

Maybe it would be more meaningful if I, or even better, a noble friend in her life would say, "I can see you are unhappy. You are going through a difficult time right now, but you have beautiful opportunities inside you and in your life. I know you don't see that right now. I would like to help you see the beauty."

Sometimes it's not about the words. Even if you find the perfect words, the person who is suffering may not be ready to hear them. It might not be the right time or place. That's what I sensed at the restaurant that day, which is why I, a stranger to her, didn't feel it was appropriate to approach her while she was with her peers.

There are many ways to offer comfort. If someone close to you is suffering and you don't know what to say, you can listen fully and compassionately. Being heard and witnessed is powerful. You can offer a hug and help them find additional resources for support. You can show them patience and love.

If it's someone you don't know, and you feel it might be inappropriate to approach and talk to this person, you can silently send your love. You can make a wish they soon will see beauty again. And you can send beauty, love, and light to them through your kind smile. I did this when the teenager glanced my way in the restaurant, and I continue to bless her with my prayers when she comes to mind. You, too, have the power to bless the people who cross your path.

Integrating Insight

1. List three things or moments that, no matter how large or small, brought you joy today.

2. Consider making this a daily practice. Perhaps each evening as you prepare for bed, you can reflect on moments of beauty, joy, or gratitude from that day. List them in your mind or write them down. Since what you pay attention to will grow, you likely will discover that the more you pay attention to beauty and joy, the more beauty and joy you will experience.

3. Is there someone in your life who is suffering now? If so, how might you show up for them as a source of comfort and a reminder of beauty?

Part Two

MORE DAILY TOOLS

How to deal with being human

Ego

5

Get Me Out of Here

I WAS A MONK with a huge ego, but I didn't know it. In fact, if you had told me I had a huge ego, I would have thought you were clueless. This is the story of how I discovered my ego problem and how I dealt with it—or actually, how my wise teacher forced me to deal with it.

When I was twenty years old, I saw myself as the greatest monk in the world. This might be a slight exaggeration, but not too much of one. I mean, why wouldn't I think that? From the time I was ordained at the age of eleven, everyone in my life literally bowed to me.

My mother, for example, went from yelling at me for my mischievous behavior as a young boy to greeting me with a full body bow, lowering her head to the floor. This is how monks are treated in my culture no matter our age.

Another way our sacredness is respected is that people don't touch us. It was forbidden for my own mother to hug me. For nearly ten years, everyone put me on a pedestal. This is the way it is with monks in my country.

I didn't realize how much it had gone to my head until I went to Australia.

When I was twenty-one, my teacher sent me to Australia to help establish a Buddhist monastery there. He had done the initial work and found a location. My job was to reach out to the local community and raise money to buy the building where the temple would be housed.

I was on my own in Australia in the middle of vast farmland. Utterly bored, I'd often gaze out the windows wondering what lay beyond the farms and fields. One day I saw a white bus come to a stop. I thought, "There's a bus! I can get out of here for a while and explore." I hurried outside and saw that the sign on the front of the bus indicated it was heading to Brisbane. I was even more excited. I was going to Brisbane. A city! Finally!

My first shock came when I stepped onto the bus and no one got up and offered their seat. This would be unheard of in Sri Lanka. Everyone in my country, whether or not they consider themselves to be religious, defers to monks. It is understood that when a monk enters a bus, he is immediately given a prime seat. In fact, it is government law. The front seats are labeled as reserved for clergy. My mind had been conditioned to this my entire life.

But when I boarded the bus to Brisbane, not one person stood up although they definitely noticed me. Everyone glanced up at the unusual sight I was—a young

Asian monk in my robe getting onto a bus in Australian farm country. I felt uncomfortable with all those eyes on me, and it hurt my feelings that no one rose for me. I immediately decided, "These people are not good. I don't like Australians."

Since all the seats were occupied, I had no choice but to remain standing and hold onto the pole to support myself while the bus bounced along country roads. My robe, which was draped around me, kept sliding off my shoulder. As I repeatedly adjusted it, I grew increasingly upset. I wanted to get off the bus, but what would I do then? I'd be stuck in the middle of nowhere, waiting for another bus just like this one.

Plus, since I didn't yet speak English, I felt particularly vulnerable. And mad. I thought, "I am done with my work in Australia. These people are mean, and they don't know how to respect a monk." Then I made up more stories about the awful Australians.

As soon as I returned from my day trip, I called my teacher in Sri Lanka. "I am very sorry to ask you this, but please send me a plane ticket so I can come home. I am done here. I want to come back to Sri Lanka because these people do not know how to respect a monk."

After my teacher gently chuckled, he said, "Okay, okay. I will do that. I will send you a ticket, but don't be in such a rush. Try to make the most of your time there."

SITTING ON THE TOOLBOX

Each day I eagerly awaited the arrival of my plane ticket, but no ticket came. I called my teacher again. Then again. Still no ticket. I finally started asking myself, "What is the problem I have in my mind? Why don't I like these people? Why do I hate Australia?"

Slowly it dawned on me. "Hmm . . . I really believe these people should treat me exactly as I am treated at home, like royalty. Well, I am like royalty. This is who I am and how I should be treated. It's not my problem these rude people don't have better manners. That they haven't been properly taught to show their respect for me in the way I have come to expect. That is their problem, not mine."

But was it? The Australians around me seemed pretty content. They didn't seem bothered or concerned with how they treated me. Perhaps it actually was my problem that I was miserable. That didn't feel good. What could I do about it?

An uncomfortable realization emerged. If I wanted my misery to end, I had to let go of my resentment that Australians didn't place me on a pedestal. I knew enough about Buddha's teachings to understand that I had become attached to being treated like I was more special than my fellow men and women—and that this attachment was the source of my pain.

Yet knowing this intellectually and feeling okay about it can be two very different matters. Perhaps you have had some experience with this in your own life. Letting go of how I expected people to treat me as a monk deeply challenged my identity. I had been a monk since I was a boy. My entire sense of who I was revolved around the fact that I was a monk. In the world as I saw it then, there was nothing more meaningful than earning the stamp of monkhood. I had done my part to earn this honor. I had pledged my life to this.

Without my identity as a monk and the corresponding ways those around me showed their respect, who would I be? I would have nothing to hold onto and no idea how to live my life. Where would I belong? It felt as if my entire identity was threatened.

This may sound a tad dramatic in retrospect, but it is how I felt as a twenty-one-year-old monk living outside his country, outside his culture, and way outside his comfort zone for the first time in his life. My teacher understood that when he laughed at me (with a monk's compassion, of course) as I insisted it was urgent that he send me a plane ticket home. He knew that my "Get me out of here!" plea was more about my need to get out of my own head than it was about leaving Australia.

I had much to learn about escaping the constraints of my ego, and my teacher gave me plenty of time to work on this. In fact, I lived in Australia for nearly five years before I journeyed further west to America.

When I arrived at the Detroit airport, a tall African American man approached me as I stood in the immigration line. He looked way down at me (I am barely five feet tall) and uttered, "Hey, man. What's up?"

He was so casual, so informal. For a moment I thought, "Really? Is this really how people in America speak to Buddhist monks?" But this time, as quickly as I felt my own negative reaction arise, I was able to let it go. The past five years had done my ego some good.

Integrating Insight

1. When was the last time you wanted to escape from a particular place or situation, although the source of your discomfort was your mindset or expectations rather than the place or people you blamed?

2. What roles in your life do you identify so closely with that you expect to be treated specially because of them? They needn't be fancy titles like doctor, lawyer, president, or CEO. They can be labels that describe your relationship status or birth order such as single parent or youngest child.

3. How might you reconsider these labels or roles so you aren't so attached to them—or at least so you aren't so attached to your thoughts about how you should behave or how others should treat you simply because of your title?

6

Checked My Ego at the Door

AFTER I HAD BEEN LIVING in America for about six months, I took a bus from Detroit, where I was living at the time, to visit friends in New York City. It was the first time I was traveling by myself on a long bus ride in America, and I was excited as I settled into my seat for the fifteen-hour ride. As the other passengers boarded the bus, they all walked past me even though the seat next to mine was empty.

When the bus driver began closing the doors to begin our journey, a teenage boy ran up and onto the bus. He made it just in time. As he strolled down the aisle looking for an open seat, he saw that the only one left was next to me.

Sitting down beside me with a perfectly straight posture, he stared directly at the back of the seat in front of him, without glancing my way or otherwise acknowledging me. As he continued to sit with a rigid back, he reminded me of a statue of Buddha. The young man wasn't moving or speaking at all.

I started feeling uncomfortable and wondered, "Is he just going to sit like a statue for fifteen hours? What if I need to go to the bathroom or get up for something? What if he won't move? Will I have to climb over him in my robe?"

In an attempt to break the silence and make things a little less awkward, I turned to him and simply said, "Hey. Hi." He replied, "Hi." That was it. No expression at all. I gently continued, "My name is Bhante. May I ask yours?" He mumbled something I couldn't hear.

After several more hours passed in silence, I was surprised when he asked me a question.

"Who are you?"

"I am a Buddhist monk."

"Why are you wearing a tablecloth?"

Wow. He thinks my robe is a tablecloth. I'd never heard that before. It showed me how very foreign a Buddhist monk must appear to him.

It also reminded me how very far away I was from home. In Sri Lanka monks' robes are revered. Unless you are a monk, you are not even to touch this sacred clothing. Now a young man is telling me my beautiful, wonderful robe is like a tablecloth. I am not enjoying this, but he asks another question.

"Are you married?"

"No, I'm not. I'm single. I cannot marry. I'm a Buddhist monk."

"You are crazy."

Of course now I know many American teenagers speak like this. They can be quite blunt. Sometimes it feels disrespectful or unkind. Back then, as an Eastern man new to this country, I reminded myself I had to adjust to the culture.

We sat in silence for the rest of the trip. When we arrived in New York, I gave the young man my card and told him he could call me if he ever needed anything. He took my card without saying a word.

I silently wished him well, knowing I had done my best. I had smiled at him and encouraged him to talk. I mindfully checked my ego at the door when I boarded the bus, and I showed kindness to someone who told me I was crazy.

Several years later, after I had moved from Detroit to Chicago, I received an email from someone named Mark. I didn't know who this Mark was, yet I noticed he used my old Hotmail address. Even after I set up a Gmail account, I kept my Hotmail account because so many people knew that address.

Still, when I saw the sender's name in my in-box, I had no idea who it was. I wondered if it was spam, but I decided to take a chance and open it. The email message was something like this, "My name is Mark. I hope you remember me. Five years ago I met you on a Greyhound bus from Detroit to New York. I don't know whether you are alive or dead. I don't know where you are. If you're alive, will you please email or call me?"

Mark's email continued, "I have some problems. That day on the bus with you I was on my way to college, to my first year at the university. I studied hard. I graduated and got a great job. The problem is, I am a drug addict.

My parents are wealthy. They have plenty of money but they can't help me anymore. They said I have to figure this out and not return home until I'm clean. They kicked me out of their house several times before. Each time, it was so difficult for me to take care of myself and stay away from drugs.

So I came up with a plan. I would go home and kill myself. As I lay down on my bed to figure out how I'd do it, I became terrified. Suddenly I remembered, 'Oh my God. I met a Buddhist monk on a bus. Maybe I can talk to him now.'"

Apparently, Mark got out of bed and began looking all over for the card I gave him when we parted ways five years earlier. That's something interesting I've noticed about American people. If you give them something, they usually keep it. I really appreciate that.

Although Mark couldn't remember where he put my card, he was determined to search until he found it. Once he located my card, he wrote me immediately. It is in my nature to respond promptly to someone who is in distress. I called and reached him right away.

"Bhante, I need help."

"How can I help you from a distance? Why don't you come to Chicago? You can stay with me."

Later that day, I spoke to my brother monk with whom I shared a home.

"I invited a stranger to our house, and he may live with us for a few months. Are you okay with that?"

"Who is this person?"

"A drug addict."

"What?! How are we going to live with a drug addict? Maybe the police will come and arrest us."

"If the police arrest us, we can practice meditating in jail."

I was kind of joking. Actually, I was nervous about what I had offered Mark, but it felt right.

My brother monk graciously responded, "Okay, okay. You are the boss. I won't complain about it."

A few days later, I picked Mark up from the airport and brought him home to live with us. I taught him how to meditate. He came with me to the many meditation classes I led. Mark was very attentive. I gave him a lot of love and care. Within this healthy environment, and thanks to Mark's strong determination to get clean, he didn't do drugs.

After three healthy months, I told Mark it was time for him to move on. Although I was confident he was ready to return to the world, he wasn't so sure. I had to push him a bit.

Mark reluctantly returned to New York City. It didn't take him long to find another good job. After that, he found a girlfriend. A few years later, Mark called to tell me that he and his girlfriend had gotten engaged, and he asked me to marry them. It was my pleasure to fly to New York to officiate for Mark and his bride. They are both happy and successful, and they are both Buddhists.

Now they have a son, who they are raising as a Buddhist. When I visited them recently, I noticed that their son's favorite toys are Buddha statues. It's so funny. Always he's playing with Buddha statues.

I remember how I thought Mark resembled a Buddha statue when he sat erect, unmoving, and silent during most of our long Greyhound ride many years ago. I am grateful that despite his seeming disinterest or disdain for me when we first met, I knew enough to keep my pride and ego in check, and to have an open heart.

I didn't give up on Mark during the bus ride or in the years since then. Most importantly, Mark didn't give up on himself. He did the extremely hard work of kicking his drug habit and building a healthy, happy, Buddhist-inspired life for himself and his family.

So much good can come when we set aside our ego and speak to strangers with an open mind, and when we try to understand our neighbors with an open heart.

Integrating Insight

1. Are you aware of the automatic judgments that arise within you when you encounter someone who is different than (or who may appear to be judging) you?

2. The next time you are in this situation, what will you do differently to keep an open heart and mind?

3. Seemingly random interactions with strangers can be profound. Have you ever experienced this? Moving forward, consider how you might positively affect the life of someone you meet (if even for a few moments) by showing up for them with an open heart and mind.

7

My Chair, Your Chair

YOUR EGO CAN BE extremely harmful. In fact, when you cling to your ego, you might become The Biggest Loser—and I'm not talking about weight loss here. I'm referring to possibly losing jobs, friends, and even family members. Do you think I'm blowing this out of proportion?

I've heard, "Sure, Bhante, people might be annoying when they are egotistical or self-centered, but is it that big of a deal? Can the ego really be that devastating?"

"Yes."

"My ego makes sure I protect what's mine, right?"

"Wrong."

Especially in Western cultures, it can be common to view the ego as essential for survival, particularly in hostile conditions. This kind of thinking assumes that the ego plays a valuable role in how we perceive and adapt to reality. Herein lies the problem. Many times I have witnessed ego-driven people turn otherwise peaceful situations into dangerous ones.

I'm not saying our egos might not be helpful in actual life-or-death situations. It's during the vast majority of everyday life that our egos wreak havoc. When you tame your ego little by little, you become happier, kinder, and more compassionate. You feel more at peace, and you can more easily give and receive unconditional love.

What is the most effective method for taming the ego? Meditation. When you mindfully observe how you look at the world, how you feel about yourself, and how you present yourself to others, you will gain insight into the ego's grip on you.

Your ego—like mine, like Buddha's—is strong. Your ego falsely believes it is the key to your very survival every day, all the time. Taming your ego is no small matter. It requires ongoing mindfulness and awareness.

If you wonder if it's worth the effort, ask yourself this: Does your ego make you happy? Perhaps it convinces you that you are better than others, but does that bring you joy? Does your ego bring you closer to—or does it stand between—those you want to be with?

Earlier I wrote about the work I had to do with my own ego when I was in Australia. Living in America for more than two decades has given me many more opportunities to continue shedding my ego. It's an ongoing process.

I have learned that the bigger my ego is, the harder it is to connect with others. If people perceive me as overly serious or prideful, they walk away. If they think I consider myself to be better than them, or if they fear I will judge them, they walk away. As the founder of a temple and meditation center, if people walk away from me because of my big ego, it isn't good for business. It isn't good for life either.

While having too big of an ego is a problem, so is not having enough of one. There are three typical directions the ego takes that can be problematic.

1. Overestimation

This was my situation. I overestimated my importance compared to those around me. I had a huge ego. People with big egos cause a lot of problems. There is no peace for anyone if you actually believe, "I am the best. I am right. We must do things my way. I will force you to do it my way if I have to."

Some people who act like they have a big ego really do have a big ego. However, other people project this image for the opposite reason. They feel insecure or unworthy, which I describe below.

2. Underestimation

This is the case with people who routinely lack confidence or courage. They think everyone else is better than they are—smarter, more attractive, funnier, happier, kinder, more successful, luckier, or something else. The list can go on and on. These people constantly compare themselves to those they encounter in real life, in the news, and on social media, and conclude they can't possibly measure up.

These folks often are lonely and depressed. Some men and women who suffer from this ego problem become withdrawn and self-defeating. Others take a different tack by overcompensating, bragging, and bullying others. This behavior ultimately is self-defeating as well. It can be tough to know if someone who behaves this way is suffering from overestimation or underestimation of their worth.

3. Misunderstanding

Some people believe, "We are all the same." Others say, "No, each one of us is as unique as a snowflake." Misunderstanding reigns. I will clarify by beginning with our commonalities. Then I'll address our differences.

According to Buddha, each one of us is made up of the four elements: earth, water, air, and fire. At the fundamental structural level, we share these basic building blocks. Our raw material is the same.

Yet as individuals, we vary tremendously in terms of our personalities, values, and behaviors. This is what makes each one of us unique. To me, "unique" feels more accurate than "different" since we are all made of the four elements.

It is very important that we try to understand and respect the qualities and nuances of one another. This is where compassion comes in. Keeping an open heart and mind is invaluable.

You may have noticed I have been writing about taming the ego, not totally getting rid of it. Why is that? For starters, I don't think that is possible or necessary. If your life is genuinely in danger, it's beneficial to firmly believe in your inherent value and preciousness as a human being. For some people, a healthy ego can help play that role.

In daily life, the ego's most useful function is to help make communication more convenient on a practical level. For example, if someone asks you who you are, the simplest, most straightforward answer might be your name. You might also say what you do for a living or where you are from. Of course these facts about you are just that—facts about you. They don't actually answer the question of "Who are you?" at a deep level, and that is okay. Most people aren't expecting those spiritual truths when they first meet you.

According to Buddhist thinking, the two different kinds of truth are conventional truth and ultimate truth. Conventional truth refers to the labels we use for our convenience, like our name or the names of objects.

Ultimate truth is the understanding that conventional truth is an illusion.

If you ask yourself, "Who am I?" you might find that you initially go to the traditional labels of your name, profession, or other affiliations. But is this the truth of who you are?

Buddha taught that "I = False Beliefs." All the labels we come up with to define ourselves are false. Why is that? Because no label can adequately capture the deeper truths of who we are as spiritual beings. Words simply point to external labels regarding our identities that we use for our convenience.

The first problem with this is that these narrow ideas about our identity (such as who we say we are and what we say is "ours") are false. The second problem is that our ego becomes overly attached to these false identifications. This happens all the time.

Let's consider something as regular as a chair. We all have plenty of experience with chairs. I frequently am invited by groups and organizations in the US, Europe, and Asia to come speak about Buddha's teachings. It is a great honor.

Whenever I walk into a temple or retreat center that I haven't been to before, the room I'm scheduled to speak in will feel unfamiliar at first. It may be lovely, with all the chairs or cushions set up just so; but still, it will feel like a new environment.

It's natural when we're in a foreign place to want to make it feel familiar or connected to us in some way. I used to do this by selecting the chair I would sit in. That way, each time I came back to that room to give a talk during my several-day visit, I could immediately return to the comfort of "my chair."

The chairs in the room would feel the same to me until I chose my chair, then that chair became special because it was mine. If that particular chair was empty and available each time I'd return, all was well. But if someone happened to be sitting in my chair when I arrived, I might feel some tension. Why are they in my chair? Do they not know it is my chair?

The tension might be subtle but uncomfortable nonetheless. Many people are creatures of habit. Do you tend to sit in the same place at the dinner table each night? Or the same part of the theater when you go the movies, or at the same place at the conference room table at work? If your chair or seat isn't available, how do you feel? This is one of the many little ways we experience discomfort when our egos label things as "ours."

Chairs are pretty minor in the scheme of things, but as I said, this attachment to what we believe to be ours can be subtle. Let's up the stakes a bit. Let me tell you the story of my new blue car.

Monks don't drive in Sri Lanka. When I left Sri Lanka for Australia and then America, people would drive me to various appointments and speaking engagements. As I received invitations to speak in more and more places, it became impractical to always have to find someone to drive me. I decided I wanted to learn how to drive. It was a modification I chose to make as a monk in the Western world.

After I got my driver's license in Illinois, I drove a used car that was not well suited for the harsh Chicago winters. Recognizing this was a problem, the considerate members of Blue Lotus Temple raised funds for me to purchase a safe new car. It was such a generous gift.

I was very happy the day I went to the car dealership and bought my brand-new blue car. I was less happy when I started driving it around town. I became so nervous it would get scratched or damaged. That night, I couldn't sleep at all. I kept going to the window to look out and make sure someone hadn't stolen my car. I quickly went from being delighted about my new car to being totally stressed out about it.

The problem was that I identified this inanimate object that lived outdoors as part of me. I wanted to protect it and keep it shiny and perfect. There is nothing wrong with taking good care of the items we own. In fact, it is responsible behavior. What is not healthy, though, is becoming overly attached to and identifying with things we call ours.

I can love my car, drive it carefully, and do my best to protect and maintain it, but that is all I can do. Someone else still might scratch or hit my car. Eventually, my car will become run down and worn out. I will not have it forever.

As soon as I accepted this car likely won't last my entire life no matter what I do, I was able to appreciate it even more. I figured I might as well enjoy it while I have it. This allowed me to relax and sleep through the night.

There is a difference between attachment and appreciation. When we overly identify with objects as ours, we may become anxious. Yet when we are grateful for these objects while they are in our care, we can feel happy and peaceful.

Let's now turn our attention from our things to ourselves. After all, nothing is more myself—more "I"— than my body. Right? Wrong. Remember Buddha taught that "I = False Beliefs." If you feel strongly that your body is "I," think about all your separate body parts. Your eyes, ears, nose, mouth, heart, lungs, hair, arms, legs, belly, hands, and so on. Imagine for a moment that you could move each part to a different location. If I pointed to the hair and asked you, "Is that I?" You would say, "No. That is hair." We could go item by item, and each time your answer would be, "No. That is not I."

Once you separate all the different parts of your body, there is no person. There is no personality. However, when all the parts are put back into form and we give the form a name, we tend to forget that the name and so-called identity are simply for our convenience. They're the conventional truth, not the ultimate truth.

Ultimately, everything is impermanent. Even if we think of our body as being solid, it is changing at the cellular level all the time. Our muscle tissues, for example, are continually breaking down and building back up. None of us will live forever. We are in a constant state of transition.

Yet we tend to cling to our conventional identities, even as we pile on ideas and belief systems. First came "I." Second came "my." Third came "mine." I call this the "I, me, mine syndrome."

When you came into this world, did you bring anything? No. You came in with empty hands. Day by day, you have collected countless ideas about who you are and what the world is about. You have become attached to your beliefs. Your ego helps secure those attachments. It happens to all of us.

When we learn to let go of the ego bit by bit, we win. We win joy, love, peace, and happiness. The more we release the ego, the more able we are to rediscover who we truly are.

Integrating Insight

1. Does your ego tend toward overestimation or underestimation?

2. Either way, what will you do to address this imbalance?

3. List things to which you are overly attached. What will you do now to loosen the reins?

Fear

8

Dealing with Fear

ONE OF THE SCARIEST THINGS I have ever done was becoming a meditation teacher in America—in Woodstock, Illinois, to be precise. I first came to the US from Australia in 1997 at the invitation of one of my Sri Lankan teachers, who asked me to help him establish the Great Lakes Buddhist Vihara in Southfield, Michigan. This monastery serves the small community of Buddhists who live in the Great Lakes region. Living and working among fellow Buddhists eased my transition to America. It was a wonderful way to come to this country.

After spending five years there and obtaining my permanent US residency, I was ready to do something different. Although I enjoyed living within a Sri Lankan community in Michigan, I wanted to assimilate into American culture. I felt called to help Westerners, who often seemed to be dissatisfied, stressed, and unhappy despite material abundance.

Although my fellow monks suggested I'd be more comfortable if I stayed in our nurturing Buddhist enclave, surrounded by people who spoke Sinhala and shared our Eastern cultural practices, I became convinced it was time for me to move on. Having heard that Unitarian Universalist (UU) churches were especially accepting and inclusive, I began sending exploratory emails to UU churches across the country. I wrote that I wanted to learn English and better understand American people and their traditions.

When Reverend Dan Larsen of the Congregational Unitarian Church of Woodstock invited me to come to rural McHenry County, sixty miles northwest of Chicago, I went. It was a shock at first. Never before had I seen so much flat farmland. The fields stretched as far as I could see. And where were the people? The area outside of town seemed deserted.

I grew up in Kandy, a large city in Sri Lanka. My first and only taste of rural life had been in Australia. While there were farms near our monastery in Australia, there also were lots of trees, hills, and a variety of vegetation. Plus, we weren't far from the city of Brisbane.

After traveling through miles of flat Illinois farmland, it was a pleasant surprise to arrive in downtown Woodstock. This small, historical town has beautiful buildings, and it was comforting to see people. Reverend Dan Larsen was kind and generous. He offered to find a local family who would host me, allowing me to live with them as I learned English and settled in.

I accepted his offer. When I moved to Woodstock, a terrific family welcomed me into their home. I was very shy. Concerned I might mispronounce the few English words I knew, I rarely spoke. It was the playful young children in the family who coaxed me out of my shell. They were so eager to communicate with me, and I knew they would not judge me. Very slowly, I began to speak more around them.

After I had been in Woodstock for several months, I was still keeping largely to myself. It was then that Reverend Dan asked me to teach a meditation class at the church.

I refused. I told him I simply couldn't do it.

"Why not?"

"Nobody can understand my English. I cannot understand them. I cannot always understand you. It is difficult for me to communicate basic things. How can I possibly teach?"

"No, no, no. They will understand. I will help you."

"I am sorry, but no, I cannot teach a class."

He kept asking me to teach. I kept saying no. But he persisted, and since he had so graciously welcomed me into his community, I felt it was my duty. Although I was terrified, I agreed to teach a class.

On a Saturday morning in 2002, I showed up in the cold, leaky basement of a church that was nearly a century old. Soon thereafter, three students arrived for the meditation class that the church had advertised.

As I sat down on my cushion, three eager faces peered at me. I was scared to death. I had no idea what to say or do, so I just smiled. They smiled at me. I smiled again. Back and forth, we smiled like that for fifteen minutes. Then I bowed to them. They assumed we were done, and they left. That was my first day of class. I never said a word.

On one hand, I was relieved. My attempt at teaching had been such a failure that there was no way anyone would return for another class. I was off the hook. On the other hand, I was disappointed I couldn't fulfill Reverend Dan's wish. I had to break the news to him.

"Reverend Dan, I am sorry I didn't fulfill your desire. I didn't know what to say to the students, so I didn't say anything. Class lasted only fifteen minutes. No one will return. I can't teach a meditation class in English. I don't know how to do it."

"I understand your concerns, Bhante, but let's try just one more time. If it doesn't work, it doesn't work. I won't ask you again."

"Okay. I will go again on Saturday, but I'm sure nobody else will be there."

The next Saturday I arrived an hour before class so I could try to relax. I was extremely nervous. Sitting alone in the church basement, I meditated. Then I began silently praying, "Please, people, don't show up. Please, people, don't show up."

That actually was my prayer. I was terrified of having to teach. After a while, I heard footsteps. When I opened my eyes, I saw the same three people from last week standing very close and staring at me.

I was thinking, "What's wrong with these people? I didn't say anything last week. Why are they here?"

The thought crept in that maybe, for some reason, they simply liked being with me. So I gave them a big smile. They smiled at me. I said a few words. I don't know what I said. I can't remember. We spent about twenty minutes together for that second class. We were becoming more comfortable with one another.

They returned the next Saturday. Soon afterward, others began joining them. When I started regularly having ten to twenty people in my hour-long class each Saturday morning, Reverend Dan asked me to teach a Monday evening class as well.

For nine years, I taught the Saturday morning and Monday evening meditation classes at the church. I grew to love it. Reverend Dan and his congregants were incredibly supportive of me. In addition to providing space in their building for me to teach classes to people who became known as the Blue Lotus Meditation Group, they even allowed me to bring in a statue of Buddha.

Reverend Dan was in his eighties by then and getting ready to retire. One day he approached me with a wild suggestion. "We are moving to a smaller location and selling this property that includes our beautiful, historic church and the two-story house next door. I would like you to buy the church, Bhante."

"I am deeply honored, but that is impossible. I don't have money to buy a church."

"You can raise the money. The members of the community will support you."

With Reverend Dan's encouragement, I began exploring this possibility with members of the church, everyone who regularly attended my meditation classes, and my friends and colleagues across the country. One woman donated $100,000. With that huge first gift, other noble friends began contributing what they could. Within a few months, we had established a non-profit organization through which we raised enough money to purchase the property.

On May 26, 2012, we held an official ribbon cutting ceremony for the newly named Blue Lotus Buddhist Temple and Meditation Center. We did this in conjunction with a Vesak Day celebration, which is the international celebration in honor of Buddha's birth.

What an incredible day it was. Several of my teachers from Sri Lanka journeyed to Illinois for the grand opening. So did most of the donors. The mayor of Woodstock officiated at the ribbon cutting ceremony, and 200 people gathered to celebrate Blue Lotus's official opening.

Given how terrified I was to teach my first meditation class in America, I couldn't have dreamed that ten years later I would be the Spiritual Director of this wonderful Buddhist temple and meditation center. The following year, I was awarded the highest honor in my lineage when I was named the Chief Sangha Nayaka of North America.

You might be wondering how we turned a historic church into a Buddhist temple. Well, we didn't get rid of Jesus.

While most church congregants were supportive of transitioning the building from a Christian church to a Buddhist temple, others were concerned that evidence of the building's rich and longstanding Christian history would be removed. They asked, "What are you going to do with the stained glass windows? And the towering statue of Jesus?"

I assured them that the stained glass windows and the Jesus statue would remain. I explained, "For nearly a decade, the Blue Lotus Meditation Group has thrived in this Christian church without any conflict. I can do that for the rest of my life."

Other than refinishing the floors and updating some paint colors, I changed very little to the historic church. Now when you enter the Blue Lotus Buddhist Temple and Meditation Center, the first thing you see is a thirteen-foot-tall statue of Jesus. Facing Jesus from the other side of the room is a nine-foot-tall statue of Buddha.

Jesus and Buddha spend every day together, surrounded by meditation, teachings, and prayer. I think they are quite happy here. As far as I know, Blue Lotus is the only Buddhist temple in the world where Buddha and Jesus sit together.

This feels right to me. Even if no one had expressed concern about losing the Christian history of the church, I still would not have removed anything of religious value. To do so would have gone against the Buddhist teachings of loving-kindness, compassion, and acceptance.

An added bonus is that many Americans, particularly Christians who are simply curious about meditation or Buddhism, feel welcomed by the somewhat familiar environment of Blue Lotus Temple.

One particular woman comes to mind. When she first came to Blue Lotus, she said to me, "I am Catholic, but I want to learn meditation. Is it okay if I face Jesus when I meditate?"

I said, "Why not? If you want to do that, please do." The first time she came to class, all of the students faced the Buddha statue while they practiced meditation, except for her. She faced the Jesus statue.

That was fine. No problem. No judgment. After a few weeks, I noticed that little by little, she began moving her meditation cushion across the room. Now she faces Buddha while she practices meditation.

I didn't ask her to convert. (I don't ask anyone to convert.) She remains Catholic, and she enjoys meditating with Buddha. I don't tell anyone what religion to observe, nor do I request that my students bow or do Buddhist chants. All I ask of them, since they come to learn and practice meditation, is just to sit down and practice meditation.

Even so, I have found that most of my meditation students now know how to chant, bow, and show respect for my fellow monks and the teachings. This wisdom came through their practice. They didn't follow what I said. They experienced it themselves.

Blue Lotus now has five Buddhist monks and one Buddhist nun who help me care for the temple and our congregation. Thanks to them, I am able to travel the world, sharing my experiences and spreading loving-kindness and joy to as many people as possible.

Integrating Insight

1. What is something you originally were terrified to do, that you now do with relative ease?

2. What is something you are still terrified to do, that you now will commit to trying?

3. Where else in your life do you want to move beyond your comfort zone?

9

Don't Live in the Garbage, Part One

S ET IN PRESENT-DAY SRI LANKA, this true story was
told to me by a young Buddhist monk I'll call Samadhi. Samadhi is very committed to living a spiritual
life. He works at the temple and does many good deeds
in the community. As is common practice, he also goes
into the village each day to collect alms.

Theravada Buddhist nuns and monks go on daily
alms rounds to collect food to eat for breakfast. This
isn't considered begging, and it differs from the Christian concept of charity in two other ways. First, no
money is given during this collection of alms. Second,
the food that is offered is intended for the community's
spiritual representatives.

Almsgiving provides lay Buddhists with the opportunity to *make merit* (do a good deed that brings benefits
in this life and the next) by demonstrating humility and
respect through feeding the monks and nuns who come
to their door. It also enables the monks and nuns to

demonstrate humility and gratitude by eating whatever food they are given.

Samadhi is one of several local monks and nuns who walk to the village for daily alms round. He is well known and well liked. Even so, there always will be people who are discontent—who look for things to complain about and people to dislike.

One such person was tucked away off the side of the road in the shade of thick vegetation drinking from a large coconut when Samadhi walked by one morning on his way to the village to collect alms. Hidden from sight and with no one else around, this discontented man hurled his used coconut shell at Samadhi, hitting him squarely on the head.

Samadhi was startled. His head throbbed. He wondered if the coconut had fallen from the tree branches above him, but when he looked down and saw that it was a used coconut, he knew this was the act of someone bearing ill will.

Rather than confront this person, Samadhi decided to keep walking. In fact, he didn't even turn his head to see who had done it. When I asked Samadhi why he didn't want to know who hit him, he offered this thoughtful explanation.

"I knew that if I looked at that person, I would carry anger for them my whole life. Instead, I chose to leave the experience right there on the side of the road. In that moment, I determined there was nothing to gain by turning around to look at the offender. I knew someone threw the coconut at me, but I didn't want to attach a face to this cruel act.

This is a small village. One day I will cross paths again with this person, and I won't know that he was the one who threw the coconut. I probably will smile and be my friendly self. I don't want his action to take that away from me.

What this man did was about his own dissatisfaction, his own mental or emotional burdens. It was not about me. I knew if I turned my body and looked at him, I would carry his burden."

As I reflect on Samadhi's decision to leave his anger on the side of the road, there is more I want to say about the wisdom of his choice in that moment. From a practical standpoint, Samadhi's decision might not be the right one for everyone everywhere. If you live in a big city and are physically assaulted, it might be very important to look at the perpetrator. Is it someone you know? A stranger? Can you describe the person clearly to the police, and pick them out in a lineup of suspects?

Those were not the circumstances of Samadhi's situation. He never thought his life was in danger, nor did he believe this onetime event was going to present an ongoing threat. All the more reason to leave this isolated incident at the side of the road.

Choosing not to look at the man was one way that Samadhi left the incident behind. Deciding not to think further about him was another. Samadhi told me he decided not to wonder about the man's motivations. He chose not to spend any time pondering, "Why did he throw the coconut at me?"

Samadhi knew it would be a waste of his time and energy to entertain those questions. The man's "reasons" were the man's problems. Samadhi didn't want to make them his problems, so he completely ignored the man.

I praised Samadhi for his insight. It takes a lot of discipline to not make up stories about other people. Often those stories are only speculation anyway. They don't get us any closer to the truth. We perpetuate angst for ourselves when we allow our minds to ruminate on the hurtful actions of others.

Samadhi's story illustrates this useful teaching: Don't live in the garbage.

* * *

Let's talk about actual garbage for a moment. When a trash container inside your home becomes full or stinky, what do you do? You take out the garbage.

I am a very tidy person. I take the garbage out often. Occasionally, though, when I come back inside, I can still detect a lingering smell. When that happens, I clean the trash container and freshen up the area.

Moving beyond literal trash, I am using "garbage" as an analogy for pain and suffering. Each one of us needs to learn how to lovingly handle and dispose of our own garbage.

The man who threw a coconut at Samadhi didn't know how to deal with his own garbage. Even so, after being struck by the coconut, Samadhi didn't put himself in the garbage.

When we ignore our pain and suffering, garbage piles up inside us. Some people have so much garbage inside that they don't know how to begin to take it out—at least not in healthy ways. This is one reason there's so much violence and dysfunction in the world.

Meditation helps us cultivate our minds so we can better understand our garbage and let it go in healthy ways. Counseling or therapy also can be helpful. Being mindful as we move through each day is important as well.

The more clearly we can see our garbage—our own history of hurts, patterns of pain, and what tends to trigger our suffering—the better able we are to deal with it without causing further harm to ourselves or others.

Consider a hot iron ball. If you know the ball is hot, you expect to get burned if you touch it. If you love yourself, you will choose not to touch it, or you will take precautions like waiting for it to cool or wearing heavy gloves for protection.

When the hot iron ball is outside you, as in the form of a cruel, toxic person, you can decide if and how you will interact with them. You may realize, "That person's anger really has nothing to do with me. They are trying to bait me with it in the hopes I will join them in their garbage. It's the same old pattern. I have tried to speak with them reasonably, but they do not reciprocate. This time I will be wise and not engage. I don't want to get burned again."

In the story about Samadhi and the coconut thrower, Samadhi chose not to touch the hot iron ball. He didn't even look at it.

But what can we do if the hot iron ball of hurt, sadness, or anger is inside us? For starters, approach it with care and consideration. Depending on the nature and duration of the pain, we might need to be gentle with it, or we might need to be firm and resolute while we lovingly release it. With stubborn trauma, we may have to try various tactics until we feel relief. It also might be beneficial to seek the support of a trained professional.

Unfortunately, a lot of people try to ignore burning feelings of shame, anger, and fear. They attempt to stuff their emotional garbage deep down, but there is nowhere for it to go. They continue hurting inside, and they hurt others.

Some people struggle with the opposite problem. Rather than avoiding their inner turmoil, they obsess about it. They keep revisiting their pain, touching it, getting burned over and over. That isn't helpful either.

We all must find a middle way. One in which we look within to understand the causes and effects. We must ask ourselves, "What is the cause of this garbage? Where is the problem coming from? How am I making the situation worse? How can I create peace in the situation?"

As we receive answers, it becomes easier to take wise action and remove garbage. I am not saying it is easy, but it does get easier. We probably all know people who seem to enjoy being miserable. They complain a lot, and they don't do much to improve the situation or themselves. The thing is, some people love living in the garbage.

We cannot do the cleaning for these people. If someone you love appears to love the garbage, you can do your best to help that person. You can ask them, "How does this serve you? How does living in the garbage help your life?"

Perhaps this will prompt them to take a closer look at the ways in which they keep hurting themselves. They may say, "You know what? I just love it. I feel more 'me' when I'm miserable." If that's the case, you can acknowledge that at least they "own" their behavior.

It's also possible they'll say, "You know what? Now that you put it that way, I realize my behavior hasn't been serving me well at all. I am ready to stop living in the garbage." This is an important first step to a more peaceful life.

Of course some fixes aren't so straightforward. Long patterns of unhealthy behavior or addiction can be quite difficult to overcome. As a friend or loved one, all we can do is our best. Bring in other support systems as well. In some situations, we might end up having to let the person live the life they choose, even if it's not what we would choose.

Each one of us has our own garbage to manage and our own life to live. Every moment of every day we are presented with new opportunities to mindfully release our garbage and be as kind and loving as possible.

Integrating Insight

1. If you were in the same situation as Samadhi, do you think you could avoid turning your head to look at the perpetrator, and perhaps more significantly, choose not to dwell on his motivations?

2. Given the circumstances, do you think Samadhi's choices were wise, foolish, or something else altogether?

3. Are there hurts from your past that you continue to dwell on—perhaps to your own detriment? If so, what are you going to do about that?

10

Don't Live in the Garbage, Part Two

TWO MONKS WHO had been best friends for many years died within months of each other. One monk was reborn as a divine being in heaven. The other was reborn as a worm in a big pile of cow dung.

The monk in heaven missed his friend. He looked all over heaven but couldn't find him. Where is my friend? Is it possible he reincarnated in the human realm? Unable to locate his friend in heaven, he searched the human realm. There was no sign of his friend there either. I can't believe he'd reincarnate in the animal realm, but I'll look there next. He searched throughout the animal realm, but his friend was nowhere to be found. Then he searched the hungry ghost realm. Finally, he checked the very low worm kind of realm.

There was his friend—as a worm burrowing into a massive pile of cow manure. The heavenly monk was in disbelief. The smell was atrocious; the environment was awful. My poor friend. I must help him. With great concern for his lifelong friend, the heavenly being knelt down in front of the stinking dung pile and yelled to the worm that had now disappeared into the manure.

"Hello! This is your best friend. We were monks who lived and practiced together. When we died, I was reborn in heaven. You have been reborn as a worm. I want to help you. I live in a beautiful place filled with divine foods and divine smells. I want to take you to heaven. Please come with me."

"Get lost. I love this dung pile. This is my home. I'm enjoying it. Why are you bothering me?"

"No, no, my friend. Let's go. You don't know what you're missing. It is so much better and nicer in heaven. You will be happy there."

"Is there dung in heaven?"

"No. No dung. No bad smells. Only pleasant aromas and delicious foods."

"If there's no dung, I'm not going."

The heavenly being and the worm went back and forth like this many times. When the heavenly being could no longer bear the horrible odor of the lowly worm realm, he held his breath, reached his arm into the pile of dung, and pulled out the worm.

But the worm was adamant about staying. So attached he was to the manure pile, he wriggled out of his old friend's hand and plunged back into the dung he called home.

* * *

I love that this story raises more questions than answers.
Here are a few.

1. Who decides what garbage is?
2. While it may be easy to look at someone else and
   determine that they are living in the garbage, do we
   lose perspective when it comes to our own mess?
3. How can we clearly see the garbage in our own
   life?
4. Is one person's dung another person's heaven?

I'll share some of my thoughts on these questions before I leave you with more to consider. As I see it, much
of this story is about the importance of leaving our
comfort zone and the value of noble friends.

It's human nature (and according to this fable, worm
nature too) to become comfortable with what we
know—even when what we know is unpleasant. Perhaps
especially then! Making changes and facing the unknown
require courage. We don't typically feel courageous or
confident when we're in a bad place. Simply put, when
we're in a dung pile, the whole world stinks.

This is where noble friends come in. According to
Buddha, there is nothing more important than a noble
friend. "Keep a noble friend next to you your whole life,"

he advised. Wise, compassionate friends provide essential perspective and support.

I have joked that another way to describe a noble friend is "a pain in the butt" because they let us know when we are living in the garbage, or when we are stuck in a comfort zone and need to make a change. Even if, and especially when, we don't want to hear it.

This doesn't mean that noble friends always succeed in their quest to help us live better lives. The heavenly monk was persistent, but the worm literally dug himself deeper into the muck. We probably all know people who are so stubborn or so fearful of change that they resign themselves to a dung-filled life. They may even convince themselves this is the life they want or deserve. That is sad.

So, is one person's dung another person's heaven? I don't think so. Not with respect to what really matters in life. Not when it comes to healthy, loving relationships. If you see a friend in an unhealthy or abusive relationship, for example, please know that they may not see the situation as clearly as you do. You may have to tell them many times that they are living in the garbage and that they don't deserve it (no one does!) before they really hear you.

Being a noble friend can be difficult. It isn't easy to open someone else's eyes and convince them they are living in the garbage. Of course, there are also many lesser ways we can get stuck in comfort zones throughout our lives. Perhaps the comfort zone takes the form of a job we stay in too long, a place we live that no longer nourishes us, or dreams and creative desires we have ignored for too long.

Life is about continual growth. Growing requires that we leave our comfort zones again and again. Sometimes we have the vision and strength to do that on our own, and sometimes we are motivated and inspired by people around us.

May you be blessed with noble friends throughout your life, and may you be a noble friend to others.

Integrating Insight

1. Where in your life are you stuck in a comfort zone or living in the garbage? If nothing comes to mind, ask a trusted friend or family member what they see that you may not.

2. Now that you or a noble friend have identified at least one area in your life where you're living in the garbage, how will you begin to dig yourself out? Then what will you do next to dig yourself all the way out?

3. Putting on your noble friend hat, is there someone in your life who you believe is living in the garbage? Perhaps you can think of many, but start with one. Decide how you can best help them clearly see and improve their situation.

Anger

11

Angry Young Monk

A S A YOUNG MONK, I had anger management issues. I really did. I had a lot of pent-up energy and frustration that I took out on others. Monasteries are typically peaceful places, but I wasn't peaceful. In fact, I definitely disturbed the peace when I acted out. It was not uncommon for me to pick fights with my brother monks.

One afternoon when my teacher approached me, I expected to get in trouble for hitting another young monk that morning. But he didn't even mention it. This is how I remember what he said and what I thought about it at the time.

"You have to learn how to love yourself, Bhante."

What is he talking about? Love myself? I don't have problems with myself. I have problems with other people.

"You must repeat these three phrases over and over: 'I am well. I am happy. I am peaceful.' 'I am well. I am happy. I am peaceful.' 'I am well. I am happy. I am peaceful.'"

That sounds silly, but I guess I have to do what my teacher says.

"Also, you must say the words out loud."

To show my teacher I was doing as he instructed, I did what he asked—whenever he was around. When I'd see him walking by, I'd say out loud, "I am well. I am happy. I am peaceful. I am well. I am happy. I am peaceful."

One day while I was repeating these phrases, the brother monk I didn't like came up and laughed at me. He said that the reason our teacher told me to repeat those words was to punish me for hitting him. I was so angry at my brother monk's taunts that I changed the words. Looking right at him I said, "I hate you. I am well. I am happy. I am peaceful. I hate you. I am well. I am happy. I am peaceful."

That is how I practiced loving-kindness in the beginning. And even when I repeated the phrases exactly as my teacher instructed, I wasn't feeling them.

If you, too, are burdened by anger, it's okay to initially "fake it until you make it" when it comes to self-love. I faked it for many years. Often anger stems from a lack of self-love. When someone doesn't feel good about who they are, anger may be a weapon they use to feel protected or strong. I recall a man I met who proudly told me, "I love anger." When I asked him why, he said he used it to control other people, especially his wife.

However, that is a false sense of power. Just because someone does what you ask to avoid your anger, it doesn't mean they respect you. Trying to control others through anger usually backfires at some point.

I understood that this man relied on his anger because he didn't have other tools to communicate and connect, and because deep down, he didn't feel good about himself. In fact I told him, "Your anger is a problem. You think it is a sign of strength, but it actually shows that you're weak. You don't have self-confidence or self-love, and you're clinging to anger as protection. Please let me teach you other tools." Fortunately, that man allowed me to do so.

On the flip side, if you are someone with a healthy sense of self, you may feel anger arise when someone treats you poorly. In that case, your anger is giving you valuable information. What you do with that information is also important.

Rarely do I suggest acting from a place of aggression. It's usually not effective anyway. It makes the other person defensive and reduces the likelihood of meaningful communication.

Instead, I advise considering what the anger might be trying to tell you about yourself or the other person. I also suggest meditating, practicing mindfulness, and offering loving-kindness to yourself and the other person. Then when you approach them, be firm and direct.

Say what you need to say while presenting yourself as effectively as possible.

Anger is a natural reaction. The next time you are angry, consider what lies underneath the emotion. Is anger arising in that particular situation because deep down you are feeling weak, insecure, or lacking in some way, or is it because you love yourself and you're being mistreated?

I can say from my own experience that as I diligently practiced self-love, my inner world kept changing for the better. That motivated me to interact differently with the outer world. When you see someone who is angry, do you tend to think, "They look so beautiful when they're furious"?

That's unlikely. A more typical thought might be, "That person looks so unpleasant." Right? Anger is ugly. Do you know what happens to your body when you get angry? That angry energy goes into your bloodstream and physical, emotional, and social problems follow.

When I was an angry young monk, I was very lonely. Who wants to hang out with an angry person? Not many people. The more I practiced loving-kindness—first to myself, then to others—the less anger I felt. The less lonely I felt. The more genuinely joyful I became.

As I became more joyful, more people wanted to be around me. I now have hundreds of dear friends all over the world. As I bring them joy, they give even more to me. My life became so much happier, richer, and better as I learned to shed my anger.

The next time someone cuts you off in traffic, you may immediately feel your blood pressure rise. What's the best way to nip that anger in the bud? Repeat these words to yourself: "I am well. I am happy. I am peaceful. Even though that driver was inconsiderate, I am well. I am happy. I am peaceful."

Allow these basic phrases to be your mantra. Turn to these phrases throughout the day, whenever needed. If others are around, you can repeat the words silently if you'd prefer.

I know thousands of people who use this mantra daily. It has changed their lives for the better, and the positive ripple effect on others is immeasurable.

Integrating Insight

1. Do you struggle with anger? If so, how do you typically manage it?

2. Have you noticed that people treat you differently based on how you are feeling about yourself?

3. If you haven't yet established a regular loving-kindness practice, now is a great time to start. Simply spend five to ten minutes each day repeating: "I am well. I am happy. I am peaceful. I am well. I am happy. I am peaceful."

12

Rescuing a Marriage

FOR SEVERAL YEARS in a row, the University of Virginia invited me to lead meditation programs during a three-week cruise for alumni. I taught a daily morning meditation class open to everyone, as well as small workshops and private sessions.

A few days into one of these cruises, a woman named Nina approached me after the morning meditation class. "I am really enjoying loving-kindness meditation. Thank you so much for teaching this. I wonder if you can offer guidance on a problem I have. It's my husband. He is a very angry man. I want to help him but I don't know how."

"Please invite your husband to come to tomorrow's meditation class with you."

"I invite Tom to join me each morning. He's not interested. In fact, he thinks it's bizarre that I attend. He doesn't understand what your class is about or why I want to get up early to do this while we are on vacation."

Even though Tom wasn't interested, Nina continued to set her alarm to arrive in time for our 8:00 a.m. class. She wasn't the only one. This was a huge cruise ship, with 700 passengers. Although many of them were still asleep at 8:00 a.m., about 200 people came to class each day.

One morning after Nina left her room early to attend class, Tom wondered, "What goes on at this meditation class? What does Nina do there? Is it some kind of cult? I need to check it out."

That morning Tom snuck into the big ballroom where class was held. He sat in the back of the room and looked out the ship's windows while I led the group in a loving-kindness meditation. He never looked at me. Just at the ocean. I don't know if he was listening at all.

I followed the meditation with a talk on the topic of managing anger. That got Tom's attention. After class, he looked for Nina but couldn't find her in the crowded ballroom. Instead, he came up to me and said, "I don't know who you are, but I really enjoyed your talk." Then he asked me a few questions, which I seemed to answer to his satisfaction. I invited him to return to class, and he said he would.

Tom was true to his word. In fact, he often was the first one to arrive. He'd bring a book, sit in the front row, and read until class began. I had no idea what was going on inside him, but he kept showing up to class.

During our closing program at the end of the cruise, I invited participants to come to the front of the room and say something about what they learned. The first people to stand up were a couple, and they were holding hands. It was Nina and Tom. Nina spoke first. She was crying, and through her tears she said, "Thank you so much, Bhante. You saved our lives."

Then she turned to face the others. Gesturing toward her husband she said, "This is my husband, Tom. We have been married for thirty years. Although we love each other very much, this marriage has been quite difficult for me. You see, Tom is an angry man.

For so many years, I've been married to an angry person. Every day I wake up to an angry person. Every night I go to bed with an angry person. I eat with an angry person. No matter what I do, good or bad, he's angry.

I recently decided that thirty years was enough. I couldn't do it anymore. A few months ago, I asked Tom for a divorce. I told him that even though I love him, I couldn't live with his anger anymore. I was ready to go my own way so I could live peacefully and die peacefully."

Tom spoke up. "Everything Nina said is true. I told her I'd respect her request to divorce, but I also asked if we could first go on one last trip together. We decided to come on this cruise for our final weeks together as a couple after three decades of marriage."

Nina continued, "We boarded the ship under awkward, sad circumstances. When I saw a Buddhist monk our first day here, I was curious. I noticed he was scheduled to teach meditation classes. I had heard of meditation but had never tried it before. It was time for me to do new things.

I was immediately hooked. The loving-kindness meditation brought me peace I have been craving. I invited Tom to join me, but he refused. When his curiosity got the best of him a few days into the trip, he came to see what I was doing each morning. Bhante's talk on managing anger struck a deep chord. Tom recognized himself in Bhante's words.

Over the past couple of weeks, Tom has fallen in love with meditation. He recognizes how much anger he's been harboring and is determined to overcome it. This is the first time in our marriage that Tom has taken full responsibility for his anger problems. He is beginning to understand the impacts of his anger on me in ways he never did before. Tom has asked me to give him and our marriage one last chance. I told him I would."

Tom added, "I will do everything in my power to make things right for Nina. I feel terrible I didn't see this with such clarity before now. Nina is beyond patient to give me another chance, and I don't want her to regret it. I am far from perfect. I still have anger. I can feel the heat of it in my body. But for the first time in my life, I also have tools and a plan. I will go after this anger with everything I've got. I will do right by Nina."

"I don't know what the future holds, but I know Tom can accomplish big things when he puts his mind to them. I am more hopeful than I have been in a very long time. I never would have believed that a new start to our marriage was possible at this point. Thank you, Bhante, for saving our lives."

All eyes were on Nina and Tom as they spoke. Many of the people, myself included, were moved to tears. We were struck by Tom's commitment to work with his anger, heal, and do right by Nina, and by Nina's willingness to let him try. We agreed to stay in touch.

Tom and Nina returned to their home in Zurich, Switzerland, as changed people. They were committed to meditation and to their growth as individuals and as a couple. They began organizing and hosting meditation retreats for their friends and invited me to lead them. I love traveling to Zurich to be with Tom and Nina, meet their wonderful friends, and meditate together.

* * *

Perhaps you've noticed in your own life that fear and anger often go together. Sometimes when we are afraid, we get angry. Sometimes when we are angry, it is because beneath that is fear.

You could say the same thing about love and gratitude. The more we practice loving-kindness, the more grateful we become. The more we focus on what we are grateful for, the happier and more loving we feel.

Here's where it gets more interesting. You can't be filled with anger and loving-kindness at the same time. Similarly, you can't be gripped by fear and gratitude at the same time. Like oil and water, they don't mix.

Buddha referred to anger and fear as weak emotions. He described loving-kindness and gratitude as qualities, or ways of being. All humans experience weak emotions. Through mindfulness and meditation, we can work with and rise above our weak emotions and cultivate higher states of being.

When we look at anger, fear, hate, disappointment, or other weak emotions and recognize them as such, they needn't hold so much power over us. I agree with Thich Nhat Hanh, "Our attitude is to take care of anger. We don't suppress or hate it, or run away from it. We just breathe gently and cradle our anger in our arms with the utmost tenderness."

Our loving-kindness practice can help us hold our anger, fear, whole selves, and the entire world in a loving embrace of compassion.

Integrating Insight

1. What strikes you the most about Nina and Tom's story?

2. Do you notice the yin and yang of love/gratitude and anger/fear in your own life?

3. The next time you feel anger or fear arise in you, try to shift to a place of gratitude, perhaps by reciting the loving-kindness mantra or focusing on something or someone you love. See what happens. Then try it the next time too.

13

Feeding Anger

A LONG TIME AGO there was a wise and compassionate king. He was a leader in the best sense—the real deal—and he was beloved. One day he had to attend to some business at the far end of the village. He told the people who worked at the palace, "I must leave for the day, and I will return this evening. Will you please look over the palace while I am gone?"

"Of course, dear King. We will take excellent care of the palace, and we wish you safe travels." Immediately they got to work cleaning, polishing, and taking great care with every item. They wanted the entire palace to sparkle when he returned.

An hour or so after the king departed, a tiny creature strode through the palace doors. It was just a few inches tall. Everyone was so busy cleaning that they didn't notice it at first. But then the ugly creature crawled up the king's throne and sat down.

The king's throne was the most revered part of the castle. Other than the king, no one ever sat on his throne. Now a filthy creature was making itself at home there. A worker in a nearby room noticed a strange, awful smell. He followed the smell to the throne and was startled by what he saw.

"Ugly, stinky creature, get off the king's throne immediately! How did you even get in here? You smell so bad. You are fouling up the palace. Leave at once!"

But the creature didn't leave. In fact, it seemed to get a little larger. The worker yelled more vehemently and hurled additional insults at the creature. With each harsh word, the creature grew a bit more.

It didn't take long for the noise and the stench to get the attention of other workers. Each one was more surprised than the next when they entered the room. Word quickly spread throughout the palace, and the room filled with people yelling at the creature, which kept growing bigger.

The workers were desperate to remove the ugly monster before the king returned, but now it had grown so large that it dwarfed the throne. It was too heavy to lift. What could they do? One worker took off his shoe and threw it at the monster. Then more shoes were being thrown, along with more insults. With each assault, the creature grew larger and stinkier. The workers were panicked.

It was in the midst of this chaos that the king arrived home. No one greeted him at the palace door because everyone was in his throne room futilely attempting to scare off the creature. Following the noise and the smell, the king stood outside his throne room and observed for a few moments before entering.

"Well, what have we here?" the king gently asked.

The workers clamored around him saying, "We are so sorry, dear King. You asked us to take care of the palace while you were away and we failed you. We have been trying for hours to get rid of this horrible, awful monster. But it won't budge, and all this time it's been growing bigger and smellier and uglier!"

The king approached the humongous creature. Kneeling down in front of it, he smiled and said, "Welcome to my home. Thank you for visiting my palace. You are so handsome. Have my people been treating you well? Would you like a glass of water or something to eat? How can we make you more comfortable here?"

With these kind words, the creature began to diminish in size. As the king continued to be hospitable, the monster continued to get smaller and its smell became less offensive. The workers were amazed.

Soon they joined in with their own loving words and actions. The creature kept shrinking until it was just a few inches tall, the same size as when it entered the palace that morning. But the workers didn't stop there.

They continued to be kind, loving, and gentle, until—poof!—the creature vanished into thin air.

* * *

I love how much wisdom Buddha packed into this story. In his version, Buddha referred to the ugly monster as "the anger-eating demon." The demon got bigger when it was fed anger, and it shrank and disappeared when it was fed love.

The demon in this story is not unlike our own demons—the anger, pain, and worries that live inside each one of us. When we treat our difficult emotions with disdain or cruelty, those feelings tend to grow. It is only when we treat our feelings with kindness, compassion, and tenderness that they might diminish or even vanish.

This applies as much to our internal self-talk (the so-called "tapes" that run through our minds) as it does to the way we speak about ourselves to other people. When we criticize ourselves or treat ourselves unkindly, we model this behavior for others. In this way, we invite more negativity into our life and the vicious cycle continues. We become angrier and infect more people with this ugliness.

When we degrade our internal environment, we degrade our external environment. Abuse, war, and other atrocities result. We damage relationships and wreak havoc on Mother Earth and the natural environment that sustains us all.

In this story, the ugly creature's horrible smell grew stronger and more pervasive. It spread throughout the palace. This reminds me of the trash and poisons we have spewed into our environment and the significant problems we now face with climate change.

Is anger really at the root of major global problems? I believe so, along with fear, ignorance, and acting from greed or misunderstanding. History repeatedly shows us how one person's bad actions can attract others who join in and similarly justify their poor behavior.

But it needn't be this way. As Buddha's story also illustrates, kind, loving, generous actions are powerful antidotes. Plus, the benefits they deliver can be contagious, growing in intensity and impact.

Pay attention the next time you feel angry or afraid, and remember that those emotions aren't bad. If you label them as bad, or label yourself as bad for experiencing them, they will be more difficult to overcome. In fact, you will be feeding them with negative judgments, much like the palace workers fed the ugly monster.

Instead, simply observe your feelings. Consider where they came from and why they are here. Do they have something to teach you, or is it time to gently or firmly pull them out from the roots and release them?

Your uncomfortable feelings provide opportunities to learn about and heal yourself. Be mindful. Perhaps practice a loving-kindness meditation. Here is one you can try when you feel anger arise.

May all beings be free from harm and danger.
May all beings be free from mental suffering.
May all beings be free from physical suffering.
May all beings take care of themselves happily.

Make amends to those you have hurt and try to forgive those who have hurt you. At a minimum, try to find peace within yourself regarding your own unkind behavior. Painful emotions and experiences can point the way to our healing. Once we heal ourselves, we are better able to help heal others and our planet.

Integrating Insight

1. Where in your life do you feed on your own anger or the anger of others? What does that look and feel like? Does it serve you and others well?

2. Seeing this more clearly, what will you do differently to reduce your suffering and the suffering of those around you? The more specific you can be, the better.

3. Going beyond merely diminishing suffering, how might you actively cultivate more peace and joy within and around you?

Grief

14

A Mother's Grief

DURING THE TIME that Buddha walked the Earth, there lived a young woman named Kisa Gotami. She was married to a wealthy man who did not treat her well. The only happy result of their marriage was the birth of a son.

Her little boy was her pride and joy. One day she took him to a fig grove to play. As toddlers tend to do, he wandered and explored around the blossoms. He found a snake, which twined around his wrist. The boy found this funny, and he laughed at his slithery friend.

As the boy playfully teased the snake, the snake opened its mouth and nipped the boy, leaving a bite-sized mark. The boy turned pale and still. At first, Kisa Gotami didn't understand why her son had suddenly stopped playing. Then she was overcome with panic.

Carrying him in her arms, she ran back to the village shouting, "Please, please, someone help me! My son was playing and now he won't move. Is there a doctor? I need medicine for my son!"

Hearing her cries, people gathered around Kisa Gotami. The toddler in her arms was dead. It was obvious. How couldn't she see this? Yet Kisa Gotami's shock was so great and her love for her son so vast, she could not fathom he was dead. She didn't believe the villagers who observed that her son had been poisoned by the snake's venom and had succumbed to death.

"No, no, he just needs medicine," she insisted. "He was laughing just a little bit ago. Look how tiny the mark is from the snake's bite. It is in the shape of a kiss. This can't possibly cause lasting harm to my son. It was just a game."

A compassionate villager who understood the mother's pain stepped forward and said to her, "There is a holy man on the hill who wears a yellow robe. Take your son to him. He may have a cure."

Clutching her son tightly, Kisa Gotami went to find this holy man. Thus it was that she found herself in front of Buddha. Trembling in front of him, she pleaded, "I was told to come to you. My son is very ill. Can you help us?"

Looking at the dead child in her arms, Buddha responded, "Yes, little sister. There is something that may heal your son. If you fetch it and bring it back to me, I can create the proper medicine."

Kisa Gotami was overjoyed. "I knew my son just needed the right medicine. Please tell me what you need. I will get it right away."

Buddha replied, "Black mustard seeds. That is all."

"Oh, that is so easy. I'll get some immediately!"

"But," Buddha added, "the seeds must come from a home that has never known death. Otherwise, the seeds will not work to cure your baby."

"Okay. No problem. I will return shortly."

And with that, Kisa Gotami headed back into town to procure black mustard seeds, still holding her boy in her arms. She knocked on the door of the first house she saw. A kind woman answered.

"My son is ill and I need black mustard seeds to cure him. Do you have any?"

"Yes, I do. I will bring you some."

When the woman came back to the door with the seeds, Kisa Gotami said, "I must ask. Has anyone in your family died?"

"Oh, yes. My grandmother died last year."

"I am sorry to hear that, but I can't take your mustard seeds. They will not make effective medicine."

At the next house, Kisa Gotami learned from the man who answered the door that his father recently died. She went from house to house. While most people were happy to give her mustard seeds, she couldn't find one home that had not known death.

Kisa Gotami was exhausted. She had gone to so many houses, carrying her lifeless son in her arms every step of the way. When the sun began to wane, she sat down on a patch of grass and looked at her cold, unmoving son.

In that moment, she realized that hers was not the only family who had faced death. In fact, there were many more people dead than living. She also knew for sure, deep in her heart, that her son was dead. She suddenly understood that her attachment to his dead body wasn't going to bring him back.

Only then could she begin to grieve. She buried her son that evening and returned to Buddha the next day.

"I am absolutely devastated by my son's death, but I want to thank you for teaching me the most important lesson. Everything that is born must eventually die."

"Dear Kisa Gotami, this is the most bitter balm. Death comes to all beings no matter how much we love them. The world weeps with your anguish. It is grief all hearts share."

Even though she was bereft, Kisa Gotami understood Buddha's message about the impermanence of life. She decided to renounce her worldly existence. Returning later to Buddha she asked, "Please, may I be your student? I want to become a Buddhist nun."

Buddha granted her wish and sent her to a community of nuns where she was admitted as Bhikkhuni Kisa

Gotami. She was hardworking and conscientious, striving diligently for spiritual growth.

One night she lit an oil lamp and sat down a short distance away. When she gazed at the flames, she saw that while some flames flared up, others flickered out. As she meditated on the flames, she considered their similarities to living beings. Some people live a long time, while others burn brightly and flicker out early.

Buddha, through his supernormal powers, observed Kisa Gotami from the monastery where he lived. He bestowed his radiance upon her and also his encouragement that she continue to meditate on the impermanent nature of everything. As she did just that, Kisa Gotami achieved enlightenment.

Buddha commented, "Though one should live a hundred years without perceiving the deathless state, yet better indeed is a single day to one who has perceived the deathless state."

Integrating Insight

1. How do you interpret Buddha's quote?

2. How might this teaching ease suffering in your own life?

3. Buddha guided Kisa Gotami to discover the truth of her son on her own. Is there anyone in your life who currently is struggling to accept something that is painful for them? If so, how might you guide them to their own discovery rather than "insist" they see or accept something they are not ready to see or accept?

15

The Tightfisted Father

THERE WAS A MAN who, despite his vast wealth, was extremely stingy. Because he never donated to charity and fiercely guarded his money, he was known as Adinnapubbaka, or "Never-Gave."

Never-Gave had one child, a son he adored. Even so, he wasn't willing to spend money on him. When Never-Gave decided he wanted to have jewelry made for his son (which was customary for people with his means), he didn't commission a goldsmith to make the jewelry because he didn't want to pay a fee. Instead, Never-Gave beat the gold himself and gave his son a pair of inferior burnished earrings. Thus, his son became known as Mattakundali, or "Burnished-Earrings."

Burnished-Earrings became very ill at the age of sixteen. Characteristically, his father didn't want to incur the expense of proper medical care. When his mother pleaded with her husband to have a physician examine and treat their son, Never-Gave refused. He said he would address the situation as he had done with his son's earrings, by doing it himself so he wouldn't have to pay a professional.

Never-Gave spoke with a few physicians and asked them how they might treat someone with his son's symptoms. Then he gathered bark from the types of trees they mentioned and samples of plants they referenced, and he created his version of a remedy for his son. But it was to no avail. Burnished-Earrings grew sicker. By the time Never-Gave relented and consulted a physician, it was too late. Nothing could be done at that point to save him.

As Burnished-Earrings neared death, his father moved him outside. He placed his dying son on the veranda, not for his son's comfort, but because Never-Gave didn't want the people who'd come to bid farewell to Burnished-Earrings to enter their house and see their possessions.

While Burnished-Earrings lay dying outside, Buddha had a vision of him and decided to visit. Along with several disciples, Buddha went to Never-Gave's home during their morning alms round. As Buddha stood outside the front door, he sent forth a ray of light to attract the attention of the dying young man.

Burnished-Earrings was deeply affected by his brief encounter with Buddha. Although he was too weak to speak, he managed to mentally profess his full faith in

Buddha. That was enough. As he passed away in pure devotion, Burnished-Earrings was reborn into the celestial world as a heavenly being.

Never-Gave was unaware that his son had risen to heaven. He was filled with remorse that his stinginess had led to the preventable death of his only child. Every evening he visited the cemetery and cried at his son's burial site. Through his tears, he sobbed and pleaded, "Please, my son, come back. Please, come back. I won't be so stingy. I won't let you die this time."

Meanwhile, from the heavenly realm, the reincarnated version of Burnished-Earrings looked down on earth and witnessed his father crying at his grave. Observing this, he decided to do something to broaden his father's perspective.

Burnished-Earrings temporarily took the form of a human being and transported himself down to the cemetery where his father was sobbing at his burial site.

In the guise of an ordinary young man, Burnished-Earrings positioned himself at a nearby grave and threw himself to the ground, wailing in anguish. His piercing screams jolted Never-Gave from his own mourning. Distracted by the bereft man in the cemetery, Never-Gave walked over and asked, "Why are you crying? What loss has caused you so much pain?"

"I have a lovely chariot, but it needs two wheels. My father promised me he would bring me the sun and the

145

moon as wheels for my chariot, but he didn't. And now he is dead. I am so sad. That is why I am crying. I am asking my father if somehow he can still deliver the sun and moon to me like he promised."

"You aren't crying because you miss your father? You are crying because he didn't give you the sun and moon before he died?"

"That's right."

Never-Gave laughed. "What a fool you are! Not to mention selfish and greedy. What your father offered isn't possible. How could he have gotten the sun and the moon just for you and your chariot? That's never going to happen. Your tears are wasted. You are crying for something foolish."

"Well, why were *you* crying?"

"I was crying because my son died, and it was my fault. Even though I have plenty of money, I was too cheap to pay a doctor for the medical care my son needed. So now, every night, I visit his burial site to apologize and beg my son to come back to life."

It was the young man's turn to laugh. "Ha! You called me foolish, but you are the bigger fool."

"I am not. Why do you say that?"

"At least I'm crying and asking for something I can see. I see the sun every day, and I see the moon every night. You are asking for something you can't even see.

Your child is gone. Crying won't bring him back. You must go on and build a new life without him."

As Never-Gave heard these words, he recognized the wisdom in them. He also understood that it wasn't so much about what can be seen versus what cannot be seen (after all, he could still clearly see his son in his mind's eye). Most importantly, he suddenly saw how futile it was to beg his son to come back to life in his old form. It wasn't going to happen. It was no more possible than expecting the sun and moon to be personally delivered as wheels for a chariot.

Never-Gave knew he would have to make peace with his grave errors—his stubborn refusal to call in a doctor before it was too late, the stingy ways that ruled his life, and the profound injustice he did to his son.

If his son could have come back, that would have eased his guilt. But Never-Gave understood that it wasn't his son's job to do that for him. Nobody could let Never-Gave off the hook but himself.

While he could still grieve the loss of Burnished-Earrings, he knew he had to find better ways to honor him and his memory. Rather than crying for his son to return, he could direct his energy to conducting an honest assessment of his own actions. He needed to reckon with and ultimately forgive himself if he wanted to move forward with a new life.

That is what Never-Gave did. He later learned that the young man at the cemetery actually was his own son who had come down from the heavenly realm to teach him this most valuable lesson. As a heavenly being, Burnished-Earrings also subsequently led his father to Buddha, encouraging him to study Buddha's holy ways and contribute his wealth to good causes. Never-Gave followed his wise son's guidance and went on to live a more virtuous life.

Integrating Insight

1. In what ways are you stingy in your own life? Being tightfisted with money is just one way to be stingy. Other ways include holding back with respect to your time, attention, energy, intelligence, or creativity.

2. How will you make amends to people you may have hurt through your inattention, withholding, or other shortcomings in generosity?

3. What specific behaviors will you change and how will you approach situations differently moving forward so that you are more generous, whether it be financially, emotionally, creatively, intellectually, and in other ways?

16

Turning Pain into Beauty

PATACARA WAS THE BEAUTIFUL, charming daughter of a wealthy merchant and banker. She lived during Buddha's time in the ancient Indian city known in Pali as Savatthi (and in Sanskrit as Shravasti). Patacara's parents were extremely protective of her. When she was sixteen years old, they put her in the top floor of a seven-story tower, with guards stationed outside to keep suitors away.

Unbeknownst to her parents, Patacara had already fallen in love with one of their servants. When they found out, they forbid Patacara from marrying him. Insisting she marry someone with equal social standing, they arranged for her to marry a young man they deemed appropriate.

When Patacara heard about the arranged marriage, she disguised herself to escape from the tower, and she eloped with the servant she loved. They fled to a village on the far outskirts of the city to begin a new life there.

Her husband farmed the land while Patacara labored diligently to cook, clean, and maintain their modest hut. It was a much different lifestyle than she was accustomed to, and although they were poor, they were happy.

When she became pregnant, Patacara pleaded with her husband to return to Savatthi with her so she could be with her mother when she gave birth to her first child, as was the custom. Patacara desperately wanted to receive her mother's love and support during the birthing process, but Patacara's husband refused. He feared that her parents would never forgive him for eloping with their daughter, and he was concerned they would torture or imprison him if he showed up at their house.

Patacara wasn't worried about that. She believed her parents would have a soft spot in their hearts now that she was pregnant with their grandchild. She was sure her parents would welcome them during her labor.

Accepting she couldn't convince her husband to join her, a very pregnant Patacara set off by herself one morning to journey back to Savatthi. When her husband returned from the fields for lunch and discovered she was missing, a neighbor told him where she was headed.

He ran and caught up with her. Although he begged her to return to the village with him, she refused. Then she went into labor and delivered their son on the side of the road. At that point, they agreed there was no point in journeying on to Savatthi, so they turned around and headed back to the village.

When Patacara became pregnant a second time and neared her delivery, she again pleaded with her husband to accompany her to her parents' home so she could give birth there. Again, he refused.

She picked up her toddler son, hoisted him onto her back, and began walking to Savatthi without her husband. Seeing her determination, he followed her. He did not want her traveling that great distance without him. Along the way, he implored her to reconsider and return home with him.

She would not. Suddenly, an unseasonal storm blew in. In the midst of torrential rain, thunder, and lightening, Patacara began experiencing birth pains and asked her husband to prepare a sheltered area where she could more comfortably give birth. He discovered a thicket with dry leaves covering the ground, and he quickly fashioned a rough shelter for their son and Patacara to settle into.

Then he went to cut down tall grasses to thatch the roof of the shelter. As he gathered grasses at the foot of a great anthill, a cobra bit him. He died instantly.

Meanwhile, Patacara labored nearby and gave birth to a second son. She was furious her husband wasn't there for her. How far could he have wandered to gather grasses? What was taking him so long?

As the storm raged throughout the night, Patacara held her children close and tried to use her body to shield them from the rain. When the sun rose and there was enough light to resume traveling, she picked up her newborn and took her other son by the hand.

She knew they must get to a warm, dry place as soon as possible, and since they weren't far from Savatthi at this point, she decided not to spend more time waiting for her husband to return.

Shortly after they began walking, they found him lying dead and rigid on the ground by the anthill. Patacara moaned in agony and blamed herself for his death. After all, she insisted on making this journey despite his pleas otherwise. She performed a ritual for her husband and bid him farewell. What else could she do but travel onward?

Now she was especially anxious to reach her parents, and she and her sons soon arrived at the Aciravati River. Due to the heavy rains, the river was swollen with fast-moving water that was waist-high. Patacara did not have the strength to carry both boys across the river at once.

She told her toddler to wait by the side of the river while she carried her newborn across. She promised to return to carry him across. The little boy dutifully waited at the river's edge.

Patacara carefully crossed the raging river, holding her newborn high above her head to ensure his safety. She set him down on a bed of leaves on the upper part of the riverbank and turned around to retrieve her other son. When she was smack-dab in the middle of the river, out of the corner of her eye, she saw a hawk. It was circling around her newborn, mistaking him for a piece of meat.

Patacara started yelling and waving her arms at the hawk to discourage it from landing near her baby. To her horror, she watched helplessly as the hawk swooped down, grabbed her newborn in its talons, and flew away.

Although her toddler couldn't see what was happening on the other side of the river, he heard his mother yelling and saw she was waving her arms. He thought she was signaling him to swim to her. As soon as he stepped into the river to make his way to her, he was carried to his death by the rushing water.

Unimaginable horror! In less than twenty-four hours, Patacara lost her husband and both of her children. As if that weren't enough, she had to witness the death of both of her sons.

Crazed with grief, Patacara cried and screamed as she ran toward Savatthi. Her parents and brother were all she had left in the world, and she couldn't get to them fast enough.

As she neared the city, she came across a fellow traveler coming from Savatthi. A hysterical Patacara told him what happened and that she was returning home. When she revealed her family's name, he solemnly told her that the violent storm had destroyed her childhood home and killed her parents and brother. Pointing at smoke rising in the distance, he said that was from their funeral pyre.

Patacara was going out of her mind at this point. She lost all sense of self and decency as she ran like a wild animal toward her birth home. She could see it had been flattened by the storm and that her family's funeral pyre was still burning.

In her deranged state, she shed her clothes and tore through the city streets shouting and screaming in agony. People pelted her with stones because they feared this crazy, unrecognizable woman, and they didn't want her to come near them.

Buddha was giving an evening talk at the Jetavana monastery, and sensing Patacara was near, he willed her to come to the temple. Not knowing why she was doing what she was doing, she ran all the way to and inside the temple. She didn't care how many people were sitting there. Naked, shameless, and distraught, Patacara approached Buddha while he addressed the crowd. He turned to her and said in a quiet, calm voice, "Sister, bring your mind. Bring your awareness right now."

Buddha's presence calmed Patacara. Her mind returned and as she looked down and became aware of her own naked body, someone handed her a cloth so she could cover herself. Buddha continued to soothe her. He assured Patacara she had come to the right place for guidance, and he said she already shed so many tears for the loved ones she lost that her tears could have filled four oceans. He wanted her to know he understood the depths of her pain.

Buddha encouraged her to focus on her own life, her own spiritual journey. Now that her entire family was gone, Patacara wanted only to become immersed in a quiet life of study, meditation, and practice. Under Buddha's care, she began her long journey back to wholeness. Eventually Patacara asked Buddha to anoint her as a Bhikkhuni. He accepted her into the order, and she went on to become one of the most popular nuns in Buddhist history.

But that is not all.

As the story goes, one night as Patacara returned home after listening to Buddha's evening talk, she washed her feet in a bowl of water before climbing the stairs to enter her dwelling place. There was nothing uncommon about this, as it was customary to wash one's feet before entering a home. She had done this exact same thing thousands of times.

But something was different this evening. Perhaps it was because she was particularly clear-minded after listening to Buddha speak, or perhaps it was because she had been devoutly studying and meditating for years by then. It may even have been because she had so fully devoted herself to the spiritual life and her duties as a nun.

Whatever the reason, that evening's ritual of foot washing led to an unusual experience. As Patacara placed one foot in her room while the other foot was still outside the door, she mindfully turned around and saw her footprints on the steps. Looking further, she watched as her footprints faded into the earth as the water was absorbed.

In that moment, the true nature of impermanence became eminently clear to her, and Patacara achieved enlightenment.

* * *

Patacara's story is well known in Buddhist lore. She was a remarkable woman who endured unfathomable tragedy and went on to live a beautiful life. She also achieved enlightenment, which is rare.

I admire Patacara's ability to transform profound suffering and pain into the deep compassion that led her to serve so many in her role as a nun. Patacara became a poet and healer, and she lived a long, fruitful life after becoming enlightened. Buddha's role in this story is that of a noble friend. I like this aspect of the tale very much. I can't overstate the importance of noble friendships.

Something else I find interesting is that Patacara didn't achieve enlightenment while meditating. Instead, it occurred as she lived her daily life, after the simple ritual of foot washing. Because she did this routine act so mindfully after spending years cultivating her mind and heart so thoroughly, great wisdom came to and through her.

Occasionally when I tell this story, someone will say something like, "If Patacara achieved enlightenment just by looking at water absorbing into the ground, maybe that will work for me as well. I can pour water into the ground, watch it get absorbed, and perhaps I will become enlightened."

Enlightenment doesn't work like that. Besides, that is a very Western, goal-oriented approach. No one achieves enlightenment by copying someone else's methods.

Enlightenment comes to those who live so fully and deeply in the present moment that they give themselves completely to the moment and to service. Patacara embodied this, and she also serves as an enduring example of someone who turned unimaginable pain into a beautiful life.

SITTING ON THE TOOLBOX

Integrating Insight

1. How does Patacara's story inspire you to look differently at the hardships you currently face in your life?

2. Patacara didn't grieve and heal on her own. Buddha gently guided her through the process. If you are grieving the loss of a loved one, who are the people (or organizations or support groups) you turn to as you heal from this loss? If you don't have a strong network of support, please reach out and create one for yourself.

3. How do you currently incorporate meditation and mindfulness into your daily life? How would you like to build on this?

Part Three

DRILLING DEEPER

Moving from surviving to thriving

Forgiveness

17

The Man Who Killed 999 People

A S THE TITLE SUGGESTS, this is a dramatic tale. It is set during Buddha's time and features extreme violence counterbalanced with profound redemption. It also happens to be full of wisdom about destiny, fear, jealousy, loyalty, personal transformation, and forgiveness.

The story begins in the middle of the night in the ancient Indian kingdom of Kosana, where a woman named Mantani had just given birth to a son. Mantani and her husband Bhaggava Gagga (who was high up in the king's court) had eagerly awaited a child for years. They were delighted.

Then something odd happened. Moments after the birth, Bhaggava noticed that the weapons the night guards around their home carried were sparkling. He had never seen anything like this before and considered it to be a noteworthy coincidence with his son's birth. Unsure whether the shining weapons were a good or bad omen, he sought a horoscope reading with the royal astrologer.

Unfortunately, the royal astrologer confirmed it was a very bad omen indeed. He informed Bhaggava that his son had been born under the constellation known as "the constellation of thieves," which would suggest he'd grow up to be a robber.

In the hopes of securing a better fate, Bhaggava and Mantani named their son Ahimsaka, which means "the harmless one." They showered him with love and wholesome values. In short, they did everything possible to raise a virtuous young man.

Their efforts appeared to be paying off. Ahimsaka was a well-behaved, compassionate child. He had an unusually strong body and a keen intellect. An outstanding student, he aspired to be accepted at the prestigious University of Takkasila.

When the time came, not only was Ahimsaka granted admittance to the university, but he also was selected to study with the most revered teacher there, Acariya Disapamuk. Ahimsaka and his parents were overjoyed. Ahimsaka loved everything about university life and made many friends. He excelled in his studies and became his teacher's favorite student. He was even invited to spend time at his home, which was not the norm. Acariya Disapamuk's wife also became quite fond of Ahimsaka and treated him as if he were the child she never had.

Life was good for Ahimsaka until the other students grew increasingly jealous of the special attention their teacher gave him. Ahimsaka's classmates began to hatch a plot to turn their teacher against him. Since they couldn't find a character flaw in Ahimsaka to exploit, they decided to make up something. They went to their teacher and told him that Ahimsaka was boasting he had become so smart that he soon would oust the great teacher. Acariya Disapamuk scoffed at their false accusations.

So the students upped the ante. They returned to him with news that Ahimsaka had seduced his wife. Acariya Disapamuk knew his wife had a soft spot for Ahimsaka, but he never suspected this. He was furious and wanted revenge. Knowing his reputation would be damaged if he personally attacked Ahimsaka, he came up with another way to hurt him. He announced to Ahimsaka that his training was now complete and that he decided what he wanted to receive for his "goodbye gift."

It was customary for students to give their teachers a special gift when their time together was over. Deeply grateful for the time he spent studying under Acariya Disapamuk, Ahimsaka was eager to learn what his great teacher desired. He was stunned, though, when he demanded, "Bring me 1,000 fingers! Each from the right hand of a different victim."

"What? Kill 1,000 people and cut off a finger from the right hand of each one? I would do anything for you, dear teacher, but please don't make me do that. I come from a nonviolent home. Your request goes against how I was raised and what I believe. Please, I beg you to consider a different gift."

His teacher insisted that was the only way Ahimsaka could properly repay him. What he didn't say, but what he expected, was that Ahimsaka would be killed or imprisoned during this quest and thereby punished for seducing his wife. With an extremely heavy heart, Ahimsaka set off to do what his teacher demanded.

I want to pause here for a moment. Often when I tell this story, someone will say they find this incomprehensible. They'll ask, "How could a compassionate young man, who is a living example of the name his parents gave him—the harmless one—plan to kill 1,000 people just because his teacher asked him to?"

Others will reference the saying I've heard American adults tell their children when encouraging them to think for themselves: "If someone told you to jump off a bridge, would you do it?"

People will protest that the story couldn't possibly be true. They find it unfathomable that Ahimsaka would blindly adhere to such an unethical and immoral request. Students of Buddhism have long puzzled over this aspect of the story. Some note that the cultural expectations to revere teachers were so immense that going against a teacher's wishes also would have been a significant violation of the values with which Ahimsaka was raised.

Others surmise that Acariya Disapamuk brainwashed Ahimsaka, while others speculate it was Ahimsaka's innate predisposition to violence (as predicted by the royal astrologer) that led him to follow through with his teacher's wishes. It has been said that Ahimsaka was a man-eating spirit with superhuman strength in a previous life, which is why he was reborn at an inauspicious time and was unusually strong. As such, despite their considerable efforts, it was impossible for his parents to raise him properly given his destiny as a robber and murderer.

But wait, Ahimsaka's story is far from done. I will return to it now so you can see for yourself what is revealed.

When we left Ahimsaka, he was on a mission to collect 1,000 fingers for his beloved teacher. He became a highwayman, killing travelers who passed through the jungle. When the people of the kingdom began to avoid the roads, he entered the villages and dragged people from their homes.

From each person he killed, he extracted one finger with his sword. He strung the fingers on a thread and hung them on a tree. When birds began pecking at the hanging flesh, he started wearing the string of fingers around his neck as a garland.

This is how Ahimsaka became known as Angulimala, which means "he who wears fingers as a garland." Quite a switch from "the harmless one"! Angulimala killed, killed, and then killed some more. When he had killed 999 people, he thought, "I need just one more finger, then I'll have done my job."

Unbeknownst to Angulimala, the king had proclaimed he was sending troops out that very day to capture the notorious killer. Soldiers were on their way to find Angulimala. This was terrifying news for Angulimala's mother.

While she wasn't sure if her son was the infamous Angulimala, Mantani hadn't heard from him in quite a while and feared that perhaps the royal astrologer was correct. If her son was destined to be a robber, perhaps he was the one who was killing people and robbing them of their fingers.

She wanted to warn him. She hoped she could save him by convincing him to renounce his evil ways and return home with her. Mantani ventured into the jungle to find her son. Just as Angulimala was reflecting on the fact that he had just one more person to kill, his mother came into view. He didn't want to kill his mother. He loved his mother. He also knew if he killed his mother, he'd certainly be reborn into the lowest hell.

Nonetheless, for a moment, he actually considered killing his own mother to fulfill his teacher's orders.

Luckily for him and Mantani, that morning as Buddha practiced his meditation, he was looking for someone to help. Seeing images of the king's troops marching toward Angulimala, Mantani searching for her son, and Angulimala considering killing his own mother, Buddha decided to intervene.

He placed himself in the jungle in front of Mantani, disguised as a regular monk. Angulimala was relieved when he caught sight of the monk. "How nice. Now I don't need to kill my mother. I can kill this monk instead."

Noticing that the monk was walking very slowly, Angulimala thought, "He moves so slowly. It will be easy to kill him." Angulimala hid by the side of the road as Buddha passed by. Then he went after him. But the strangest thing happened. Strong and mighty Angulimala was running as fast as he could, but somehow he couldn't catch up to the monk. How could this be?

Tired and exhausted from the chase, he yelled out, "Hey, monk, stop! Don't run. Stop."

Buddha turned around with a smile and replied, "I am not running. I am walking. You are the one running."

"I cannot reach you, monk. I cannot reach you. You must stop."

Buddha said, "Now I have stopped. You must stop."

Angulimala was angry and flustered. "You can't possibly be stopped. I am running but I can't reach you."

"That is because your 'stop' and my 'stop' are two different things."

"What does your 'stop' mean?"

"Mine means that I have stopped doing all the negative, bad, and violent things that hurt myself and others. I have stopped doing those things, but you haven't stopped. That is why you are exhausted. Your discontent keeps you in a constant state of motion."

Buddha continued, "Even when I am walking, I am calm and still inside because I don't harm or kill. You can't stop. You can never be still as long as you harm and kill."

This made perfect sense to Angulimala. In that moment, he dropped his weapons, fell at Buddha's feet, and begged for mercy. "Monk, please take me as your student."

"Okay. I will. But we must go to the temple right away because the king's soldiers are nearly here and they will kill you."

Buddha took this murderer to the temple and immediately ordained him. The moment he was ordained, so moved was he by Buddha, Angulimala entered enlightenment. In fact, he may have been the only former criminal in Buddhist history to be ordained and become enlightened on the spot.

But his story isn't over yet.

The next morning as the soldiers set out again to find and capture Angulimala, the king joined them and led the way. As they passed the Jetavana monastery on their way to the jungle, the king requested they stop there first so he could pay homage to Buddha.

When Buddha saw armies of soldiers arrive with the king, he asked, "Why are your armies here in full force? Has a war been declared?"

"No. We are not at war. I have gathered all my men to capture the infamous Angulimala."

"What if I told you that Angulimala is now a bald-headed monk who intends to do only good?"

"That's impossible. There is no way such an evil, violent man could suddenly transform into a virtuous, humble monk."

"Oh, but he has. There he is, meditating over there."

The king was visibly shaken. He couldn't reconcile the horrific stories he heard about Angulimala with the quiet, meditating monk.

Buddha gently said to the king, "There is no need for you to be alarmed. Angulimala has been transformed. He will not cause further harm. You can go talk to him and ask him yourself."

So the king did. When he spoke with Angulimala, he asked about his family. After Angulimala told him the names of his parents, the king remembered them and the terrible omen his royal astrologer revealed when Angulimala was born. The king also remembered the compassionate, intelligent young man Angulimala used to be before he strayed so horribly.

Buddha assured the king that Angulimala was now his student, and that he was determined to redeem himself. With that, the king led his troops away from Angulimala, sparing his life. Although the king was willing to pardon him, the townspeople were not. When Angulimala went on his morning alms round, the villagers threw stones at him. He returned to the temple with a bloody head and no food.

Buddha said, "Don't do alms collection for a few weeks. I will bring you food until this tension goes away. You must stay inside. This is your *karma*."

Angulimala understood that even Buddha couldn't release him from the karma of his murderous ways. That would take time, a deep commitment to a virtuous life, and forgiveness. After many months as a devout practicing monk, during his morning alms round, Angulimala was approaching a house when he heard the cries of a woman in agony in labor. He immediately stopped collecting alms and hurried back to the temple.

"Buddha, I just came from the home of a woman who is experiencing intense labor pains. Please, tell me what I can do to help her be more comfortable."

Buddha told him to return to her house. "Stand in front of it. Don't go in. From outside her home, chant this powerful prayer in her name to give her a better birth."

Buddha proceeded to instruct Angulimala to chant these words: "Sister, since I was born I do not recall intentionally killing a living being. Through this truth may there be well-being for you and well-being for your fetus."

Angulimala said he didn't feel right saying those words since they were untrue. He had killed so very many people in his lifetime.

Buddha then offered this modification: "Sister, since I was born with the noble birth (became a monk), I do not recall intentionally killing a living being. Through this truth may there be well-being for you and well-being for your fetus."

Angulimala promptly returned to the woman's home and chanted this blessing over and over, standing outside her front door. The woman safely gave birth to a healthy child. When word spread that Angulimala's blessing aided in this child's healthy birth, many towns-people took that as a sign that Angulimala had truly transformed. Up until then, he was still hated by many of the people in the kingdom. They had closed their windows and doors to him and refused to give him alms.

Yet even his success in blessing this mother and child wasn't enough to win the favor of all the townspeople. Angulimala continued to be attacked by angry mobs. He never fought back because he accepted this was the karma he brought upon himself through the murders he committed. He felt he deserved this punishment.

Angulimala continued to punish himself in other ways as well. He was regularly tormented by visions of the people he had slaughtered. He rarely found inner peace. Even his meditations were interrupted by the horrible memories of what he had done.

The only thing that brought him a modicum of relief was chanting on behalf of the laboring woman and her child. While he chanted and focused fully on a healthy outcome for them, he forgot himself for a little while.

Thousands of years later, monks still use Angulimala's chant to bless pregnant women and their developing children. In fact, I did this chant for an expectant mother just the other day. It is timeless.

* * *

There is much we can learn from Angulimala's life. I'll recap several of the story's main themes.

1. Power of the Mind
The mind is incredibly powerful. As a boy and young man, when Angulimala focused his mind on his studies and living a virtuous life, he was exemplary. He then turned to evil with the same vigor, before returning to redemption with the strength and determination he

brought to his previous endeavors. These later efforts led to his monkhood and ultimately sainthood.

It is also worth noting that even good people can go astray under the influence of charismatic people with bad intentions. This is another reason to always keep noble friends close. They can provide essential perspective.

2. Possibility of Transformation

According to Buddhist teachings, there is no such thing as original sin or permanent sinners. We don't tell people, "You are wrong. You are a bad person." Instead we focus on their actions, and we offer compassionate, steady guidance to help them return to a healthy, virtuous path if they stray. The extreme nature of Angulimala's crimes, combined with the fact that this murderer became a saint, suggest that even the worst offenders can be rehabilitated.

3. Accountability

Angulimala was held accountable for his murderous ways—by Buddha, by the townspeople, and by himself. This is karma (*kamma* in Pali, but since most Westerners are familiar with karma, I'm using that version here). Angulimala's story reminds us that karma is inescapable.

While karma must be repaid, it is up to each person as to how they choose to respond to their karma and change their behavior. We are always interacting with our karma. Karma responds to our actions and vice versa. We can change the course of our lives through mindful, skillful living. No one is predestined to a life of evil or doom. We exert much influence over our future. This relates to the two themes above—power of the mind and possibility of transformation—as well as the one below, forgiveness.

4. Forgiveness

Angulimala struggled mightily to forgive himself, and he suffered deeply because of his inability to do so. Focusing on others by chanting to the mother giving birth provided a brief reprieve from his self-flagellation.

If you suffer from low self-esteem, depression, or the inability to forgive yourself, I suggest you first do everything in your power to apologize and make amends to the people you have wronged. This should be a deeply felt and thoughtful process.

If your wrongdoings are significant, this will take concerted effort and attention. And if the person or people you mistreated are no longer alive, you still can write or speak to them as if they were living.

In addition to doing your best to make amends to the people affected by your actions, I recommend volunteering, service work, or other ways of paying it forward with your time and resources. As Angulimala experienced, tending to others is a gift to the giver and receiver alike.

Of course I also suggest that you cultivate your mind, taking a careful look at your behavior and your reactions to other people's behavior. By better understanding yourself, you can make wiser, healthier choices moving forward.

Integrating Insight

1. Forgiving ourselves can be one of the most difficult things to do. Where or with whom in your life do you wish to be granted a fresh start? What must you do to make amends to the person or people you have harmed? If you have already fully made amends, what is stopping you from forgiving yourself?

2. Do you believe in karma? How would you describe your perspective on it and its role in your life?

3. As you reflect on the conversation Angulimala and Buddha had about running versus stopping, can you personally relate to being in constant motion or continually keeping yourself busy or distracted to avoid underlying discomfort? If so, what pain are you running from?

18

Granting Forgiveness

MANY PEOPLE TELL ME the word *forgiveness* feels heavy to them, full of religious connotations and often tied to the concepts of sin and redemption. Others worry that only God can pardon their transgressions, and that their life or afterlife hangs in the balance. With all due respect if these are your beliefs, I view forgiveness differently.

In Buddhist teachings, forgiveness has little to do with others. It is more about your relationship with yourself. Let's say, for example, that a husband and wife are unhappily married. After many years of difficulty, they get divorced. Yet they remain angry and don't know how to forgive.

The wife comes to me and says, "Bhante, even though we've been divorced for many years, I'm still furious. Every time I think about my ex-husband, I get upset and mad. When will this end?"

"It won't end until you forgive yourself."

"Forgive myself for what? He's the bad guy. Let me tell you all the terrible things he did."

"That's not necessary."

"But it is. If you knew how he behaved, you'd understand why I can't forgive him. Then maybe you could help me feel better."

"If you really want to feel better, you must learn to forgive yourself."

"I still don't understand. Forgive myself for what? I tried so hard in our marriage. I did the best I could."

"I am sure you did. Maybe your husband did the best he could as well. Maybe he did the best he was able to do, even if it didn't work for you."

"Well, then his best was pretty awful."

"Maybe so. But what your husband did or didn't do is done. It's in the past. How long are you going to keep hurting yourself by carrying around the past and rehashing it?"

"I don't want to do it anymore. That's why I need your help."

"And that's why I am telling you that you won't be free of the pain until you forgive yourself. You can forgive your husband or not. You can see that he did the best he could with the tools and knowledge he had, or you can believe he didn't do his best. Either way, it doesn't matter. What matters is that only you have the power to stop hurting yourself now. To let go of the pain, you must forgive yourself. You alone hold the key to your contentment."

"But what am I supposed to forgive myself for? For remembering? For carrying around the hurt?"

"You remember what you remember. There's no need to forgive yourself for your memories. But must you dwell on them? Does continuing to focus on the past hurt or help you?"

"I think it might remind me not to get involved with someone like my husband again."

"Do you really need that constant reminder? I am sure you learned plenty from your marriage and your divorce, and you will continue to learn, but not by holding onto past grievances. That will just keep you stuck, feeling sad and bitter.

If instead you treat yourself with compassion and remain mindful as you meet new people, you probably won't repeat past mistakes. You'll also be more likely to attract people who are able to treat you as lovingly and compassionately as you treat yourself.

When you sit quietly and look into your heart, you will discover what you need to forgive yourself for. Perhaps it's for choosing to marry someone who couldn't love you well (even if you didn't mean to choose that), or for staying in an unhappy marriage for so long (even if you thought you were doing it for the right reasons), or for carrying around the hurt for so many years after your divorce (even if you believed it would protect you from future disappointment)."

* * *

The reasons to forgive are personal and unique to each situation. Forgiving need not be reserved for atrocious sins, like with the previous chapter's Angulimala, the man who killed 999 people.

Forgiveness often is about acknowledging we are human beings with good intentions *and* flaws *and* blind spots. Even with good intentions, we will make mistakes. We will wish that some relationships turned out differently than they did. But they didn't.

In the end, there is little we can control. The best we can do is appreciate we are here to grow and learn, and let go of what no longer serves us. You are the only one who can do that for yourself. Through forgiveness and self-love you can set yourself free.

Maybe you're thinking, "I understand why it's useful to forgive myself for how I've been hurt in the past, especially if I was a child or otherwise vulnerable at the time. I also know I can look only to myself to heal from injuries caused by someone who is no longer living. However, what should I do if I'm currently in a relationship where my partner continues to mistreat me? Where does forgiveness fit in, and what about accountability?"

I am glad you asked! Forgiveness and accountability are quite related. I'll offer the example of a different couple here. Dan and Mary came to me as many couples have because they wanted to find out if their marriage could survive infidelity.

Dan is an artist and stay-at-home father to the couple's two young daughters. Mary works in finance and travels frequently for her job. Married for nearly a decade, they had drifted apart. Mary became intimate with one of her coworkers during several recent business trips.

Wracked with guilt, she told her coworker that their brief affair was a terrible mistake, and she ended it. She said she loved her family and needed to make everything right with Dan.

Dan was devastated when Mary told him she cheated on him. He absolutely did not see it coming. Although life had been very stressful lately with the demands of raising the girls and Mary traveling often for work, Dan viewed their lack of closeness as temporary. He never questioned their marriage, and he certainly never imagined this.

Dan and Mary were emotionally raw when they came to see me. Dan had been sitting with Mary's confession for a couple of weeks by then, and neither one looked like they had been sleeping much. My heart went out to them. Dan's pain was palpable. So was Mary's. She was filled with remorse, apologizing over and over to Dan for hurting him and for jeopardizing their family and the life they built together.

While we discussed the strains in their marriage that led to *but in no way justified* Mary's affair, there were a lot of tears. I italicized that phrase for a reason. It was not my place to judge whether or not the affair was "justified." It was Mary's. Mary—and Mary alone—had to take full responsibility for her choices and their consequences.

She did. This doesn't mean it will be easy for Mary or Dan to do the hard work of healing themselves and their marriage, but it was a crucial first step. Forgiveness will play a big role moving forward. Mary must forgive herself for her transgressions. She also needs to continue expressing her remorse to Dan, and she must back up her apologies with consistent evidence of her changed behavior. She needs to make amends in ways that matter to him.

Dan has to forgive himself for being blindsided. In the immediate aftermath of Mary's confession, he blamed himself for being naïve and missing the signs of serious distress in his marriage. That is a miserable blame game to play, as it only adds insult to injury.

I helped Dan understand he was not to blame. He's a loving, trusting person who doesn't have a crystal ball. None of us do. Because Mary took full responsibility for her actions, she helped Dan understand that the fault lied in her, not in him. Although Dan and Mary still have a long road ahead, they are committed to learning from this and rolling up their sleeves to do the important work of forgiving.

What if Mary hadn't been genuinely remorseful? What if she tried to relieve her guilt by blaming Dan in some way for her actions? I have seen plenty of men and women do that. It's a defense mechanism some people use when they find it too painful to face what they've done. However, the inability to assume accountability is a relationship killer.

A healthy relationship should be reciprocal. Not every moment of every day, but certainly over time. If one person keeps behaving carelessly or unkindly, and the other person keeps forgiving them (even if they genuinely feel compassion for their partner), it degrades the relationship.

I have counseled loving, openhearted people who find it easier to forgive their partner than to take good care of themselves. I remind them of something I learned the hard way, something that's become a personal motto. *My loving-kindness is not my foolishness.* I write much more about this in the chapters that follow.

For now I want to continue on the topic of forgiveness, while also bringing anger into the discussion. At first Dan was mostly shocked, hurt, and sad that Mary cheated on him. Then he became enraged as he thought more about how he had been holding down the fort at home as a devoted husband and father, while his wife slept with another man at fancy hotels.

When his anger began eating him up, Dan came back to see me. "Bhante, Mary is doing and saying all the right things now. She feels horrible about cheating on me, and while I don't think she'll do it again, I am so angry. I keep picturing her with the other man, and I can't seem to move on. I am furious with her. Can you help me?"

After I told Dan I understood he was really hurting, I said something he didn't want to hear. "As tempting as it may be, don't make Mary the bad one."

"What do you mean? She chose to cheat on me. She has taken full responsibility, just as you advised. How can you now say this was somehow my fault?"

"That's not what I am saying. Mary is completely responsible for her actions. You are not at fault. However, the poor decisions she made with her coworker are only a part of who Mary is. If you focus only on her transgressions and not on how much she loves you, how good she is with your children, and her many other wonderful qualities, you will remain stuck in a rut of anger and despair.

It is dangerous to cast Mary as the bad one and you as the good one or the victim. No one can win in that situation. You are understandably hurt and angry. Forgiveness will take time. It's not a onetime event; it's a process. Right now I encourage you to focus not on Mary but on yourself. How can you care for yourself during this difficult time?"

"What do you mean?"

"What are some kind and loving things you can do for yourself? Perhaps treat yourself to a massage, or a bike ride with the guys, or a babysitter so you can have a chance to relax when you've been caring for your daughters all day and Mary is out of town."

"What should I do when the anger comes up again? Even if it goes away for a little while, it always comes back."

"You might not like what I'll suggest next, but it works. Sit with your pain. Don't try to hurry it along. It takes time to heal. Right now your anger is deep-rooted, like a tree. If you try to make it go away by chopping down the tree in the middle of its trunk, it won't work in the long run. The tree will grow again unless you take out the roots. Be patient.

This is not an easy process, but it is doable, and that is why self-care is especially important right now. Sit with the pain when you can, attend to your daughters when they need you, and make time for yourself to relax and heal by doing things that feel good to you. Even a short walk in fresh air can make a difference.

Also, please don't compare your experiences with grieving, healing, and forgiving to anyone else's experiences. Not to Mary's and not to someone who claims to know exactly how you feel. Many people have spouses who have been unfaithful, and there is no shortage of advice on how to deal with it. But only you know what is in your heart and what is right for you and your family.

For your marriage to survive this, you and Mary both need to do your own work. Of course all you can control is your side of the equation. No matter what Mary does, you must do your work and take care of yourself.

If Mary continues to do her work, great! If she doesn't keep doing her work, maybe you will decide to walk away. No matter what, releasing your anger and forgiving is your job. Your forgiveness is first and foremost for yourself."

Integrating Insight

1. Who have you been struggling to forgive?

2. Do you typically find it easier to forgive yourself or others? Are you now clearer on the importance of self-love and forgiving yourself? Most of us need to learn how to forgive ourselves for the "flaw" of being human.

3. Of the many ways others can hurt us, betrayal—being violated by someone we've loved and trusted—can be especially brutal. Have you experienced a betrayal that you have not yet fully recovered from? If so, what takeaways from this chapter will you apply to your healing journey?

19

Beyond Forgiveness

FORGIVENESS IS A TOUGH ONE. People often suffer greatly because they are unwilling or unable to forgive others for the ways they've been hurt. Let's face it. Humans are sensitive beings. There are countless ways we may feel slighted, misunderstood, mistreated, or worse. Sometimes the person who hurt us isn't aware they've caused pain, or if they are aware, it's not what they intended.

That's not to say there aren't people who lack compassion, or those whose limitations keep getting in the way of better behavior. There *are* people like that. Sometimes we are related to them. Deciding how to manage (or walk away from) relationships with those people might be an ongoing aspect of our own spiritual practice.

Difficult people have always been around. In the Aghatavinaya Sutta, Buddha spoke of five ways to deal with feelings of anger that arise when dealing with a troublesome person. The first three suggestions—to develop good will, compassion, and equanimity regarding the person—relate to practicing loving-kindness. The fourth suggestion is to ignore the person.

Buddha's fifth suggestion is that we remind ourselves that the bothersome person is the product of his or her actions and will bear the ultimate consequences. "This venerable one is the doer of his actions, heir to his actions, born of his actions, related by his actions, and has his actions as his arbitrator. Whatever action he does, for good or for evil, to that will he fall heir." In other words, the difficult person creates and carries their karma (as we all do), and ultimately will be held accountable.

I have found this fifth suggestion to be particularly helpful in tricky situations. In fact, I recently referred to it while trying to resolve a sensitive issue with a long-time colleague who I'll call Marshall. Marshall worked with me, helping with my classes and various other matters. While I appreciated Marshall's efforts on my behalf, he also had a tendency to be controlling, which I found challenging at times.

For a while I thought I was handling things well, but then it got to the point where I had to admit to myself that the relationship was not working. Although it wasn't easy to do, I let Marshall know that I didn't want to work with him anymore.

Marshall was disappointed. He asked if we could meet to try to resolve our differences. I said I'd love to do that, thinking that if we could talk about our concerns openly and honestly, it could be very beneficial. We set a date to get together, but thirty minutes before we were scheduled to meet, Marshall called to cancel. He said he didn't want to talk about our challenges.

I said, "I understand. It's okay. You are a longtime Buddhist practitioner, as am I. We both know the dharma, our practice, and our journey. We both believe in karma. One day, karma will address this. Perhaps you and I have done all we can for now. We don't have to force a conversation if you're not comfortable with it. We can just let this be, knowing that karma will somehow take care of it."

Marshall agreed, and we went our separate ways peacefully. I share this personal story to clarify something about Buddha's fifth suggestion. It can be tempting, especially if you're currently angry with someone, to interpret it with an "edge" or bias, as in, "Karma will bite that bad guy back! He'll get what he deserves!" But as I said to Marshall, and as he and I both believe, karma goes both ways. Each of us gets our fair due.

We each bear full responsibility for our words and actions. Perhaps you can recall a situation in which you and another person saw things very differently, yet you both felt you were "right." Or perhaps you recall a scenario that wasn't a black-and-white matter of right or wrong. While neither party did anything "wrong," there were hurt feelings and unresolved issues because you and the other person had fundamentally incompatible personalities. When there isn't a clear case of someone who's right and someone who's wrong, what happens then with karma?

My example with Marshall fits this description. With respect to how karma addresses this, I'll say that I believe in my practice. I believe in my actions. I am fully responsible for my actions and how I care for myself and my life. I spoke and behaved as best I could with Marshall while also respecting my own well-being. Marshall likely did the same. That is why our work together (for now at least) is done, and we can trust whatever karma arises from our interactions.

I want to clarify that karma doesn't mean "punishment," as many Westerners seem to believe. Rather, it means "action," and it's the intentions behind our actions that lead to favorable or unfavorable results.

You will encounter all kinds of people throughout your life, including those who aren't as aware or mindful as you. If you sense up front that a person is not someone you want to do business with or engage socially with, you can keep your distance, knowing it's not healthy or fruitful to spend time and energy with someone who's not the right person for you.

But you'll also meet people whose weaknesses or limitations aren't immediately obvious. They may be charming, charismatic, and attractive. They may say and do the right things initially. Even if you typically are an astute judge of character, they may slip past your radar. Only after you have become heavily involved in a personal or business relationship, do their true colors emerge.

Perhaps they stop taking responsibility for their actions and begin doing things that harm you. Even after you talk with them about this, they persist in mistreating you. They refuse to take responsibility or even try to see things from your perspective. Since you've already become emotionally or financially invested with them, it can be harder to accept that this is just who they are.

You likely will feel hurt, disappointed, even confused. You may question yourself for getting involved with them. You may grieve. You are human, and so are they. No one is perfect. Learning to live with imperfections—our own and others—is part of life. It gives us plenty to work with in our loving-kindness practice, and often more than we want to deal with when it comes to practicing forgiveness.

But if practice doesn't make perfect, it does make things much better. As someone who has been practicing loving-kindness and forgiveness for more than forty years, I can definitively say it is a practice *and* a process *and* it works.

These days I rarely find myself wanting or needing to forgive someone. This is not because people never mistreat or try to take advantage of me. Even though I am a monk, or perhaps because I am monk, this still happens.

The difference is how I deal with it. As I wrote in the previous chapter, forgiveness has less to do with others than it does with our relationship to ourselves. Because I have been practicing loving-kindness for so long and because I continue to engage in a daily mindfulness practice, I have an excellent relationship with myself.

In accordance with my personal motto that *my loving-kindness is not my foolishness*, I keep my distance from or ignore certain troublesome people, as is Buddha's fourth suggestion in the Aghatavinaya Sutta. The less I engage with them, the less opportunity there is for them to hurt me, and the less I later must forgive!

Still, I occasionally become involved with people who have gone on to treat me poorly. Right now, I am thinking about someone in particular. A longtime friend from Sri Lanka, who I found out was lying about me and saying unkind things about me behind my back.

Since I had believed he was a good friend, I was quite surprised and upset by his actions. As soon as I learned what he was doing, I confronted him. When he looked me in the face, he told more lies and refused to show compassion or take responsibility. What came out of his mouth is what some people refer to as BS and what I call garbage.

I asked myself, "Why am I getting into this man's garbage? I have a wonderful life with beautiful opportunities. Why would I get into those stinky garbage cans with him?"

The choice was clear. I decided to walk away from that friendship. Although I say the choice was clear, it wasn't easy because we had been friends for a long time. In fact, it was really hard on me in the beginning, but once I let it go, I felt tremendous relief. More than relief, I experienced complete resolution. Once I released my hurt, it was gone for good.

Occasionally mutual friends will bring him up and make a reference to something he did or said about me in the past, and I honestly don't remember what they are talking about. They ask me, "How can that be?"

All I can say is this: "I discovered that once I fully released the hurt, it was gone. The details don't matter. In fact, I can't even remember them. I feel light and free. Even memories no longer burden me."

This is what it feels like to move beyond forgiveness.

Integrating Insight

1. Has it ever happened to you that someone reminds you of an injustice done to you in the past, but because you've done the work to release it, it no longer resonates for you?

2. If so, what did you do that enabled you to move beyond forgiveness?

3. If not, is there a troublesome person or situation you now want to release? What new insights from this chapter will you use so you can experience the freedom and joy that come from moving beyond forgiveness?

Loving-Kindness

20

Loving-Kindness is Not Foolishness

A COBRA WHO LIVED in a forest near a monastery happened to quite enjoy listening to the monks chant. As he observed them meditate, he noticed they seemed to be so peaceful and content. Curious to learn more, he slithered up to a monk one morning, bowed to him and asked, "What exactly are you doing?"

"I am reciting a loving-kindness meditation."

"Will you teach me how to do this?"

"Sure. It's easy. Sit cross-legged and keep your back straight."

The monk waited for the cobra to arrange the lower part of his body in a cross-legged fashion and straighten his back. When the cobra was well positioned, the monk continued. "Repeat the following words to yourself: 'I am well. I am happy. I am peaceful. May all beings be well, happy, and peaceful.'"

"That's it?"

"Yes, that's it. Repeat this many times. Allow yourself to feel the meaning of the words. You can practice this meditation as often as you like. When you are calm and relaxed, and when you are not. It can be especially useful during times of difficulty. Any time is a good time for loving-kindness meditation."

"Thank you, kind monk. I am so happy to learn this. I think I'm going to really like doing a loving-kindness practice."

The cobra bowed to the monk and slithered away. True to his word, the cobra began regularly reciting the loving-kindness meditation. Sometimes he did it silently, and sometimes he said the words out loud. He loved it. He always felt relaxed, peaceful, and calm whenever he practiced. He also noticed that these wonderful feelings typically remained with him for quite a while.

After he had been meditating for a few months, an elderly woman with poor eyesight wandered near the cobra during his morning practice. The woman was looking for firewood. By the time she approached the cobra, her arms were overflowing with sticks and branches she had collected. All she needed was a rope to bundle them up with so she could drag the firewood home. Her arms were tired and she was ready to be done with this chore. Due to her failing eyesight, she mistook the cobra for a rope.

She grabbed the cobra and used it to tie up the firewood. The rough edges of the branches jabbed into his body as she wrapped him tightly around the wood and used the remaining length of his body to tie a knot. Then she proceeded to drag the bundle the long way back to her house. The cobra was in agony. He was getting cut and bruised, scraped and pinched. What could he do though? He had been training so intently with loving-kindness, and he remembered the monk told him that the loving-kindness meditation could be especially useful during times of difficulty.

This certainly qualified. He silently recited, "I am well. I am happy. I am peaceful. May all beings be well, happy, and peaceful. I am well. I am happy. I am peaceful. May all beings be well, happy, and peaceful."

But then—wham!—the cobra was banged into a large rock protruding from the ground. "This is crazy," he thought. "I am not well, happy, or peaceful. This old lady is hurting me terribly. I do not wish her well. What was that monk talking about? This isn't helping at all."

The cobra was miserable, not to mention angry. Angry at the monk for teaching him something that wasn't good. Angry at himself for believing in this practice. And angry at the old woman for hurting him.

Finally, they arrived at the woman's home. She untied the bundle and tossed aside what she still believed to be a simple rope. The cobra painfully slithered away from her and headed straight to the monastery. He was seething.

He sought out the monk immediately. He didn't bow this time when he approached him. "Look, stupid monk, because of you I have suffered greatly. I trusted you. When you told me how wonderful loving-kindness practice is, I believed you. Look at me now! I am torn, bruised, and bloody. I have been used and abused. Yet I didn't harm anyone—neither before nor during this whole ordeal. I just tried to practice loving-kindness. Now I am wounded. What a mess. This is all your fault!"

The monk began to laugh. This made the cobra angrier. "Why are you laughing at me? How dare you?"

The monk said, "I am sorry to tell you, but you didn't practice loving-kindness. You practiced foolishness."

"No. I practiced loving-kindness just as you instructed. I repeated the exact words you said. I didn't cause any harm to the lady, but she harmed me a lot."

The monk explained, "Even when you practice loving-kindness, if someone mistreats you, you must speak up. That is your duty. People aren't always aware when they cause harm. If you suffer at the hands of another, you must let them know. They can't read your mind. So speak up, but do it with compassion. You are a cobra. All you had to do was hiss. It's okay to hiss. You can hiss without releasing poison.

By the way, dear cobra, you are not alone. Human beings must learn this lesson as well. This is why I say to
them, 'A regular loving-kindness practice can help train
you away from reacting from anger. But if you are mistreated, speak up. Take care of yourself. Say what you
need to say without anger and without poison.'"

Integrating Insight

1. Are you in the habit of speaking up promptly when you are treated poorly, or do you tend to let resentment build until you explode with poisonous words?

2. Can you think of a current situation that's troubling you or of a person with whom it's time to have an honest, compassionate conversation about what's not working and how to make it better?

3. Moving forward, how will you ensure that you practice loving-kindness but not foolishness?

21

Loving-Kindness is Not
Being a Doormat

SOMETIMES LOVING-KINDNESS doesn't look like loving-kindness. Sometimes it looks like anger. But even if it looks like anger, it's not. Let me explain.

I was teaching a full-day retreat at the Blue Lotus Temple on the subject of Love in Action. The students and I were enjoying lunch together in the meditation room after a full morning of teachings and loving-kindness practices. The mood was relaxed and open.

A drunk, homeless man stumbled in. I recognized him immediately. He regularly hangs out near the temple, and I have interacted with him many times. Although he always asks for money to buy milk, it's evident he uses it to buy alcohol. I do not judge him and I often give him spare change.

At first I simply observed as he intruded on our peaceful lunch break. One by one, he began approaching the students and asking for money. A few people reached into their purses or wallets and gave him money. Others apologized to him that they didn't have money with them.

Everyone was trying to be kind. After all, the theme of the retreat was Love in Action. I continued to watch as he became more persistent with a woman who said she had no money with her. She looked over at me, clearly uncomfortable.

It was time for me to step in. In a strong, firm voice, I said, "Get out of here right now!" The man immediately stopped hassling the woman and turned toward me. Gazing directly at him, I raised my voice again and said, "Get out of here! Now!"

He looked stunned. He took a few uneven steps, turned around, and walked out the door. My students were shocked. Prior to that moment, they had only seen me speak quietly, with a kind and gentle tone. They viewed me as a peaceful, compassionate monk. Now they had witnessed me yelling—at a homeless man no less!

The woman he had been pestering was the first to speak up, "Bhante, why did you do that? Why did you yell at that man and send him away? I am confused. This is a class on Love in Action. What's going on here?"

I replied, "Even though this class is about Love in Action, it's not okay to allow people to mistreat you. He was mistreating you, and he was mistreating the temple. That is not okay."

"But did you have to be so harsh with him?"

"I did. I know this man. I have given him money and offered support before, and I will do so again. I also know him well enough to know that my words would not have been effective with him if I delivered them in a gentle, weak, or pleading tone. I had to be firm."

I explained that I chose my words and tone to match the situation at hand. Had we been interrupted by someone who was sober and with whom I could have a reasonable conversation, I would have responded differently.

"But, Bhante, you were so angry."

"I wasn't angry at all. I was simply acting angry. There is a huge difference. I made a strategic decision. In that situation, with that particular man, I decided that the most loving way I could care for you, me, the temple, and even that man, was to deliver a forceful command."

One of the other students spoke up, "Bhante, I get why you did what you did. I understand how it helped our classmate who was being badgered, and how it supported our class as a whole and the temple, but how were your actions helpful to the man? How can yelling at someone be considered compassionate, peaceful behavior?"

"Great question, my friend. I believe I demonstrated compassion for the man by giving him extremely clear feedback on his behavior. In Western psychological terms this is known as 'drawing a clear boundary.' By doing so, this man now knows not to waste his time or energy by behaving this way again in our temple. He understands he will need to behave differently if he wants a more pleasant, positive reaction."

"Okay. But did you really need to yell at him? Could you have been firm and clear using a gentle voice?"

"Sure, with some people that's effective. I didn't believe it would have worked with him, though, especially in his drunken state. Also, while I understand you think I was 'yelling,' I think of 'yelling' as coming from a place of rage or fear or cruelty. I wasn't coming from any of those places. Yes, I raised my voice, but I did so from a place of loving-kindness."

I continued, "Love in Action is not about allowing other people to mistreat you. If you allow others to do that, you are in trouble. If you let others misuse or take advantage of you, you are not being loving toward yourself. In any given situation, there are various factors to consider and many ways to love yourself and others.

Loving-kindness may wear different faces, but it is never about weakness. It is about the quality of the mind, and as such, it is the opposite of anger."

Integrating Insight

1. What is a recent situation in which you felt unsure about what the "right" or "loving" thing was to do?

2. Do you typically consider your own needs or primarily other people's needs when you practice loving-kindness?

3. If you tend to forget or discount yourself, how might you ensure you care better for yourself in the future? Remember, loving-kindness is not being a doormat.

22

Loving-Kindness Begins
with Yourself

ADDRESSING THE MONKS gathered before him, Buddha spoke of a famous acrobat known for his talent as a performer and his teaching ability. He attracted many admiring students. One day the acrobat was invited to perform in the center of the town's marketplace. Knowing there would be a large audience, he wanted to impress the crowd with a bold trick.

He decided to ask one of his top students if she'd like to assist him during the upcoming performance. "Of course! I would be honored to assist you." She was so excited that she didn't ask him any questions. She simply agreed to meet him the following morning to prepare for the big show.

When the acrobat awoke the next day, he thought, "The trick I have in mind is very dangerous. There will be no safety net. I should make sure my young assistant is okay with assuming this risk."

As soon as she arrived for their rehearsal, he asked, "Do you know what I have planned for us? This new trick that is sure to wow the audience?"

"I have no idea what you have in mind. But you are the best acrobat in the land, and I am excited to work with you. I will do whatever you ask."

The smart, experienced acrobat wanted to get that in writing. He asked the assistant to sign a contract agreeing to follow his instructions precisely. Although she was eager to work with him, she also had an intelligent mind of her own. "If you'd like me to sign a contract, I first need to know what you want me to agree to. What is this trick you'd like me to perform with you?"

Pointing to a long bamboo pole, the acrobat said, "I am going to balance that bamboo pole on top of my left shoulder. Your job is to climb up the right side of my body, cross over to the bamboo pole, then climb up the bamboo pole and balance on top of it. During the performance, I am going to take care of you, and you are going to take care of me. That is our contract. Please sign here."

As honored as she was by this opportunity to perform with the acrobat, the young woman took a deep breath and kept a clear mind. She respectfully replied that she needed a bit of time to consider the contract before signing it.

"Think about it if you must, but I'll need you to sign and bring it back to me very soon because the show is this afternoon."

After a short time of careful thought, the young woman returned to the acrobat and said, "I am not comfortable with the way this contract is written. May I suggest a change?"

"What do you have in mind?"

The assistant marked up the contract so that it said, "During the performance, I will take care of myself, and the master acrobat will take care of himself."

"That is the opposite of what I proposed. I said I will take care of you, and you will take care of me."

"I can't agree to that. I will agree to take care of myself, and you must take care of yourself."

At this point in the story, Buddha turned to the monks and asked, "Which contract is better? The acrobat's or the assistant's?"

Some of the monks said the acrobat's contract is best; others said they preferred the one by the assistant.

Buddha applauded the monks who sided with the assistant. He pointed out that she understood when we take care of ourselves, we take care of the world.

* * *

How is this true that when we take care of ourselves, we take care of the world? Using the acrobat's daring trick as an example, what qualities in addition to skill are necessary to succeed? Trust. Loving-kindness. Surrender. Balance. Mindfulness.

Both the acrobat and his assistant must focus on cultivating these qualities within themselves to best support themselves and the other. They each need to direct their attention within first.

Consider the alternative, which is what the acrobat proposed. What if the assistant was tasked with attending first and foremost to the master acrobat? If she became overly concerned about him, she might get distracted and lose her own balance. If she lost her internal focus and balance, even for a moment, she'd be in danger and she'd also be putting him at risk.

This goes both ways. If the master acrobat was excessively worried about his assistant and made a mistake, he'd endanger them both. That is why each person must take full responsibility for their own actions, for being mindful, and for taking care of themselves.

By caring for yourself, you can best care for others. Loving-kindness begins with yourself.

Integrating Insight

1. It is one thing to say, "Loving-kindness begins with myself," and it is another thing to believe deep down that it's true. At this point, do you feel any resistance to this teaching? If so, what is it?

2. What does "loving-kindness begins with myself" look like in your life? Name specific ways you live in alignment with this teaching.

3. Are there relationships or situations in your life that need some adjusting so you can better live in accordance with "loving-kindness begins with myself"?

23

Eleven Benefits of Loving-Kindness

THE METTANISAMSA SUTTA is a wonderful teaching Buddha delivered to a gathering of monks at the Jetavana monastery. *Metta* means loving-kindness. *Anisamsa* means benefit. Combining the two, this sutta identifies eleven benefits of loving-kindness. This is my modern interpretation of Buddha's famous words about the advantages of a loving-kindness practice.

1. You sleep comfortably.

My experience in America is that many people suffer from poor sleep. I frequently hear complaints about insomnia and other sleep problems, most of which I attribute to what I call the wounded mind. As we discussed earlier, when your mind is wounded, you may be filled with anxiety, fear, anger, disappointment, and self-loathing. These toxic emotions pervade your nights as well as your days.

When the emotional fire of angst burns throughout the night, you will not sleep well. However, when you regularly practice loving-kindness, you will better understand your needs as a human being made of light, and you also will become more skilled at letting go.

The world is not perfect. Neither are you nor are the people in your life. Everyone makes mistakes. The key is learning how to forgive and how to cease constant worrying.

You won't automatically become loving and kind when you recite the words, "I am well. I am happy. I am peaceful." But when you regularly meditate and practice mindfulness, you will gain insight into your resistance to being loving and kind to yourself and others. You will more clearly see your expectations and the false beliefs you cling to.

With this clarity, you can choose to release what doesn't serve you. As you shed these burdens, you genuinely become more loving and kind, you feel freer and lighter, and you sleep better.

2. You wake up feeling rested.

This second benefit naturally flows from the first. A good night's sleep enables you to wake up feeling rested and joyful. This is significant. Feeling good when you awake sets a positive tone for the entire day and helps perpetuate a healthy cycle.

Consider the opposite. When you wake up feeling unwell, how does that affect the rest of your day? Perhaps you are grumpy and short-tempered with your family and coworkers. You don't think clearly and you make poor choices. This leads to having more things to worry about and to repair.

It is far more enjoyable to begin each morning feeling well and reaping benefits throughout the day and night.

3. You rarely have bad dreams.

People often tell me about the nightmares that awaken them. As with poor sleep, bad dreams frequently are the result of a wounded mind. When your mind is filled with negativity, so is your dream life.

A daily loving-kindness practice will help you sleep better and more peacefully. That is not to say you will never have unpleasant or fear-based dreams. Some dreams provide important warning signs about potentially dangerous people or situations. In those cases, it is wise to heed your dreams. Take appropriate action to protect yourself and your loved ones.

The more you practice loving-kindness, the less you will experience negative, fearful dreams. This makes it easier to discern which frightful dreams offer valuable wisdom to apply to your life.

4. You are attractive to others.

When you regularly practice loving-kindness, your body relaxes and your face becomes joyful. This tends to draw others to you.

When I was an angry young monk, I had few friends. The more I practiced being loving and kind to myself and others, the happier I was. I smiled often and became relaxed, clear, and open.

I now have so many wonderful friends all over the world. Being with them brings me joy, and I am able to spread this joy to others. Together we fuel a beautiful cycle of love and kindness.

5. Animals are attracted to you.

Animals can sense loving-kindness. I love dogs. Just the other day as I sat outside and meditated, a dog came up and licked my face. Its owner was quite surprised. She explained her dog is usually fearful of human beings so this behavior was very unusual.

It didn't seem unusual to me. Dogs and cats are always coming up to me. I know it is because of my loving-kindness practice. Animals can feel a compassionate heart and good intentions. These qualities help animals feel safe. Don't be surprised if you attract more animals as your loving-kindness practice expands.

6. Divine and celestial beings guide and protect you.

We may never know the many ways that divine and celestial beings protect us. Sometimes they offer guidance as we dream, pray, or meditate. You may have noticed that the more relaxed you are, the more receptive you are to messages and insight from beyond our earthly realm. In contrast, when your mind is clouded with fear, anger, or anxiety, it is difficult to tap into deeper wisdom.

Many spiritual traditions equate spirit with breath. To "inspire" means both to "inhale" and to "be guided by the divine." I love connecting with the divine through breath, meditation, mindfulness, and loving-kindness.

7. Fire, poison, and swords won't touch you.

What does this mean? How can loving-kindness offer this degree of protection? This seventh benefit is best understood symbolically. Buddha famously said there are three kinds of poisons—greed, hatred, and delusion. He also spoke of the fire of greed and of verbal daggers that can skewer peace.

From this perspective, it makes sense that a strong loving-kindness practice can inoculate someone from poisonous mindsets and needless suffering at the hands of others who exhibit these qualities. Since like attracts like, when you are internally clear and peaceful, you are more likely to attract others who are as well.

8. Your mind calms and focuses easily.

With a regular meditation and loving-kindness practice, your mind can settle into meditation and more readily concentrate as needed in everyday life. This applies as much to focusing on work as it does to dealing with a difficult person. When you are calm and peaceful, you aren't easily baited by someone else's garbage. Since you aren't quickly angered or thrown off, little or no recovery time is needed after an unpleasant interaction. Because your perspective helps you move through life with a more even temperament in general, you needn't ride an emotional roller coaster.

9. You embody loving-kindness.

You may have noticed these benefits are deepening as they progress. In the Pali translation of this teaching, both the fourth and ninth benefits make reference to the face and body becoming more joyful and peaceful as a result of practicing loving-kindness. In the fourth one, it is said that this draws other people to you. The ninth benefit declares that your entire countenance becomes serene—your face and full physical complexion brighten and exude love.

This is how I explain it during my loving-kindness workshops. I say that through a regular practice, your inner light turns into loving-kindness. Your light and loving-kindness cannot separate. Your eyes become loving-kindness. Your words become loving-kindness. Your face becomes loving-kindness. Your smile becomes loving-kindness. Your touch becomes loving-kindness.

I end my loving-kindness workshops by going to each participant and placing my palm on top of their head as I bless them. This is another way to directly spread the energy of loving-kindness. Of course I am not the only one who does this.

Throughout history and across cultures, spiritual leaders face their palms toward people as they offer blessings. In Eastern countries, we bring our palms together and bow. First, we go inward. We internalize everything first through our loving-kindness practice. Then we bring our palms together and point them outward to give back.

When we embody loving-kindness, we are vehicles of love. Through our palms, eyes, words, faces, and smiles, every act can be one of loving-kindness.

10. You will die with a clear, peaceful mind.

Many people fear death. I have noticed that people with troubled relationships and unresolved conflicts become particularly agitated and unsettled as death approaches.

Just as practicing loving-kindness can help us enjoy a clear and peaceful mindset throughout our lives, it can do the same in our final moments. When we approach death with a genuinely deep sense of peace, this is comforting not only for us but also for our loved ones.

11. You will be reborn into a peaceful place.
Even if you haven't reached enlightenment upon your death, you still will go to a very peaceful, loving, and wonderful place, be it the divine realm or a better human realm.

Integrating Insight

1. Which of these eleven benefits do you currently enjoy, and how does this impact your life?

2. Which of these eleven benefits seem to elude you, although you may long to experience them?

3. What other benefits have you enjoyed or do you anticipate enjoying through a regular loving-kindness practice?

Mindfulness

24

The Good Remains

THERE WAS A YOUNG KING during Buddha's time named Mahanama. He was a devout follower of Buddha, and he worked diligently to cultivate his practice and his mind.

After spending the day listening to dharma talks and meditating at the temple, King Mahanama was walking back to his palace. The streets were filled with people, music, and dancing on this fine summer evening. King Mahanama couldn't help but notice the beautiful women all around.

However, as soon as he saw his attention going toward the women, he became concerned and thought, "I was focused all day as I listened to the dharma and meditated. I was so happy at the temple. But the moment I saw all these beautiful women, I got distracted. I am not a good man. I am disappointed with myself."

The next day he returned to Buddha and told him about his experience. "Buddha, I am troubled by my wandering mind, and I'm concerned about something else as well."

"What is it, Mahanama?"

"What if I were to die on the way home from the temple one day? What if I left the temple with a pure mind, became quickly distracted like I did last night, and then was struck by a runaway elephant, horse, or chariot? If I were killed during a moment when my mind was muddled, what would come of me? Where would I be reborn?"

"You will be fine. You won't be reborn into a bad place. You need not worry about that."

"You are the Great One. You are so wise, but how can you be sure? Last night I was easily distracted."

"That's okay. The important thing is you didn't behave badly. You are committed to cultivating your mind and behaving with virtue. Don't be so hard on yourself. You are a good man with good intentions and a regular practice. It is the nature of the mind to wander. You are doing your best."

King Mahanama felt himself relax and breathe more deeply as he listened to Buddha's reassurances. Buddha continued, "Imagine if a jar of oil was thrown into a deep lake. The glass would shatter when it hit the rocks at the bottom, and the oil would rise to the water's surface. Your good deeds are the same.

As long as you continue to cultivate your mind with study, virtue, and discernment—no matter how you die or what happens to your body afterward—your inner goodness will rise to the surface. Your noble actions will be rewarded with a favorable rebirth. The good remains."

* * *

As I tell my students, distractions come and go. That is the nature of the mind. Yet I also remind them about their inner goodness. The Buddha-nature that dwells within each one of us is more enduring than passing distractions.

A related Buddhist teaching offers a simple analogy about the weather. It's so basic that even a young child can understand it. It goes like this: "On dark, gloomy days, where is the sun? Has it been extinguished? Is it gone forever? Of course not. The sun is there even when we can't see it, even when it hides behind the clouds."

Our fears, worries, and anger are like the clouds. Even when they distract us, even when they are all we can see some days, the light of our inner Buddha-nature continues to shine behind the clouds. Just as clouds can't extinguish the sun, distractions and mistakes can't extinguish your inner light. Your goodness remains.

Integrating Insight

1. Do you beat yourself up about your practice or how clear you can keep your mind afterward?

2. If so, does this story provide a useful perspective?

3. Can you think of someone who tends to be very hard on themself and with whom you can share the story of King Mahanama or the simple analogy about the weather?

25

Seeing Distraction

IN THE LAST CHAPTER, we talked about not being too hard on yourself when you notice your mind is distracted. Now we're going to take this a step further by looking at how you can actually use distractions to help you become more loving and compassionate toward yourself.

This story is about a monk who was deeply into his spiritual practice and his search for peace. As he sat under a tree meditating one day, Mara appeared. In Buddhist traditions, Mara represents the unwholesome states that keep us bound up in daily suffering, such as our inner critic, desires, and fears. Mara is a demon whose sole purpose is to wreak havoc on those around him. While some say Mara was a man who existed in physical form, others think of Mara as a troublesome state of mind. In modern terms, Mara might be described as a negative mindset.

In this story, Mara saw the earnest monk meditating and thought, "If this monk cultivates his mind well and becomes a peaceful, positive influence on others, I will lose some of my power and will be less able to sway people into evil ways. I know what I must do. I must distract him."

Mara began to violently shake the tree that the monk was sitting under. The monk was pelted with falling leaves and small branches. And since there was no breeze that day, the falling debris took the monk by surprise, jolting him out of his meditative state.

"I must clear away these leaves and twigs before I can return to my meditation." After he mindfully raked the area, the monk situated himself under the tree again and closed his eyes.

This did not please Mara. "What? He's at it again? I need to come up with another distraction." This time Mara disguised himself as a cow and circled around the tree releasing mounds of dung. The foul smell of fresh dung roused the monk from his deep meditation. Opening his eyes, he was quite motivated to remove the piles of manure. After doing so, he sat back down and resumed meditating.

Mara thought, "Really? The dung wasn't enough? I must devise a better distraction." Disguising himself as an old man, Mara pounded a walking stick and made noises all around the monk. The monk was becoming suspicious at this point. "Why am I having so many distractions today? What is really going on?"

As the monk considered the circumstances, he had an epiphany. These weren't coincidences. This must be Mara's nefarious handiwork. Confident in his realization, the monk declared, "I see you, Mara!"

The jig was up. Now that Mara had been seen and called out for what he really was, he couldn't continue to hide. He appeared in front of the monk in his regular form, and the monk said, "Mara, you are a powerful being. You can do anything. Your abilities to distract are incredible. May I request that you do something for me?"

Mara's ego was stoked. Absorbing the monk's flattery, he responded, "I *can* do anything. What would you like me to do?"

"Can you disguise yourself and appear in front of me like the real Buddha?"

"Hmmm. I've never been asked that before. That's a good one. I might not be able to appear one hundred percent like the real Buddha, but I could probably appear ninety-nine percent like him."

"You truly are amazing, Mara. I would love to see that. Will you please do it for me?"

Buoyed by his compliments, Mara reappeared in front of the monk as a peaceful, living Buddha. When the monk focused intently on the Buddha before him and started meditating, he attained enlightenment.

* * *

Modern life is filled with distractions. I love how this story encourages us to approach distractions with an open mind and as a way to further our own spiritual journeys.

I am using the word "distractions" broadly to include unpleasant emotions and mindsets, such as jealousy, greed, anger, desire, fear, rumination, self-flagellation, and so on.

I find it beautiful that as soon as the monk recognized he had been allowing Mara to distract him, he named what he saw. He identified and articulated the problem with, "I see you, Mara!"

But naming the problem is just the first step. The next step is to look inside for clues about why we might have been particularly susceptible to Mara in that moment. And to explore our weak spots, poor habits, and vulnerabilities. This is what we do when we practice mindfulness and observe ourselves daily during meditation.

Seeing and naming Mara took away his power. Once he was called out, Mara was forced to appear in his regular form. Similarly, when we recognize and name our fears and hurts, we remove their power. As we develop the ability to regard our full selves with warmth and compassion, we are better able to do the same for others.

Good triumphs over evil in this story. The monk represents purity of spirit and intention. Mara represents evil. The monk uses mindfulness and ingenuity to transform Mara's negative inclinations into a force for good. Enlightenment was an unexpected bonus—and a grand one at that.

Integrating Insight

1. Viewing Mara as the embodiment of negative mind-sets, how does Mara tend to show up in your life? Put another way, what tend to be your common mental or emotional challenges—being jealous of others, worrying obsessively, engaging in other self-defeating behaviors, or what else?

2. The next time you witness one of these negative patterns or triggers emerging, look inward and see what shifts if you declare in the moment (silently or aloud), "I see you, Mara!"

3. Once you've seen and named the specific aspect of Mara that appeared, take a deeper look at the pattern. Why were you triggered this time? What underlying, unresolved issues can you now begin to address?

26

The Circle of Life

IMAGINE WALKING AROUND and around in a big circle.
You can't see what lies beyond the circle. You can
only see directly in front of you and directly behind you.
You think the circle is the only way to go. In Buddhist
teachings, we call this *samsara*, which means wandering.

I think many of us are like a group of blind people
walking endlessly in a samsaric journey. We don't see a
beginning or end to the wandering, but we want to
believe there is a purpose, a "method to the madness" so
to speak. Since we don't fully grasp what it may be, we
keep walking with blind faith that there is something
more. More meaning. More clarity. But what happens as
we keep walking this circle? We get tired. We get upset.
We get mad.

The circle contains pain, difficulties, and delusion.
This suffering and dissatisfaction is known as *dukkha*,
and the process of samsara is described as the repetitive
cycle of birth, death, and rebirth.

Picture that one day as we walk the samsaric circle together, a wise woman questions, "What are we doing? What is happening here? We are looking for the beginning and end of this circle but they don't exist, and we keep bumping into disappointment, confusion, and frustration. The real answer is to step outside the circle and see it for what it is—our conditioning, our conditioned minds."

This realization is liberating. Since this astute woman understands we are conditioned by society, she begins to shed her conditioning. Motivated to slice through delusion, she looks inward to discover what feels true for her in each moment.

Her blinders are off. She now can choose if and when she wants to walk the circle with the rest of humanity, but she no longer will do so blindly. She is not attached to the circle. She understands it's a man-made construct.

Each one of us can cultivate the ability to become a witness through meditation. By carefully observing ourselves and the world, we can develop a healthy perspective on the circle.

By the way, the circle isn't to be viewed solely as the cycle of physical birth, death, and rebirth. It also encompasses the many stages we go through in the course of a lifetime. We can choose to shift perspectives and reinvent ourselves along the way. By accepting that our outer reality is a projection of our inner reality and that what we may have thought of as our permanent self—our ego, personality, body—isn't so fixed after all, we can be reborn in each mindful moment.

That's not to say it is easy. No one is immune from the hard knocks of life, be they physical, intellectual, financial, or emotional. Growing up isn't smooth sailing. We all experience loss and heartbreak.

Buddha understood this well. He once asked his monks, "Which do you think is greater—the water in the oceans or the tears you've shed while wandering?"

His answer was "the tears." Buddha suffered plenty. Suffering inspired him to find a way to break out of the monotonous cycle of samsara. Samsara is a process, not a place. I will talk more in the next chapter about Buddha's prescription for breaking free of samsara, but for now I'll say it's basically about allowing ourselves to let go of our resistance to life. Only then can we experience contentment.

I view contentment as being more solid than happiness. In America I hear many people say, "I just want to be happy," or "All I wish for my kids is that they are happy." But to me, happiness is just another aspect of the conditioned mind. If we are conditioned to believe that something will make us happy, we fantasize about it. We may even obsess about it. We equate happiness with pleasure. When you eat ice cream, you may say, "I am happy. This is so good." Since happiness is about pleasure, it tends to be superficial and fleeting.

Contentment is a more enduring satisfaction and knowing. It comes from a healthy perspective on the samsaric journey and an ability to appreciate life's joys and sorrows. Contentment arises when we allow our minds to become unconditioned—when we shed the illusions of our conditioned mind. Contentment comes from within; happiness is fed from without.

The moment Siddhartha attained Buddhahood, he was filled with sublime joy and contentment for what he realized under the Bodhi tree. It has been said that these are the first words he uttered, in fact sang, when he became enlightened as Guatama Buddha.

Through countless births in samsara,
I have wandered without finding
The housebuilder I was seeking.
Born and suffering again and again.
Oh housebuilder, now you are seen!
You will not build the house again.
All your rafters have been broken,
And the ridgepole has been destroyed.
My mind has reached the unconditioned,
And craving's end has been achieved.

This is Buddha's declaration that he was free from suffering. He had reached *nirvana*. The house represents our bodies, our conditioned minds, and our desires, defilements, and suffering. The housebuilder is each one of us. We create our own problems.

Buddha recognized that our psychological, emotional houses are constructed from ego, desire, and delusion. By breaking the rafters and destroying the supporting structure, we can release suffering and limitation. By becoming unconditioned, Buddha was free from the compulsions that propel many of us mindlessly through life. Have you ever felt you were just going through the motions?

The first step toward enlightenment is self-awareness. When we train ourselves to observe and be mindful, we remain connected to the people around us without becoming so easily triggered.

Consider the lotus flower. Rooted in muddy water, the lotus flower rises above and offers its beautiful blooms to the world. Although the lotus flower depends on mud and water for its very survival, its precious blossoms don't get bogged down in the muck. Nor need you.

Integrating Insight

1. Do you live like a lotus flower? Are you able to remain rooted in earthly experience and relationships without becoming easily disturbed by the words or actions of others?

2. When you notice you've lost perspective on the bigger picture of life and what really matters to you, how do you bring yourself back to a clearer, more accurate space?

3. Do you recognize the distinction between happiness and contentment in your own life?

27

The Middle Way

PRINCE SIDDHARTHA GUATAMA was born into a life of luxury more than 2,500 years ago near the border of present-day Nepal and India. His mother, Queen Maya, died shortly after giving birth to him, and his father, King Suddhodana, doted on him.

King Suddhodana went to great lengths to shield his son from the miseries of the outside world. Prince Siddhartha was raised within the confines of the palace property, and royal life was all he knew. He was taught by esteemed teachers and trained in archery and martial arts. He ate the finest food and was entertained by the most talented performers.

But over time, this didn't feel like enough. Siddhartha longed to explore what lay beyond the palace gates. In an effort to keep him bound to home, the king arranged for Prince Siddhartha to marry a young woman who became known as Princess Yasodhara. They were sixteen years old when they wed.

As they awaited the birth of their first child thirteen years later, a restless Siddhartha convinced the driver of the royal chariot to take him on an excursion. They hadn't traveled far when they encountered a frail, old man.

Siddhartha had never seen an elderly person. The sight shocked him.

"Does this happen to everyone?" Siddhartha asked the charioteer.

"Does what?"

"Looking like that. Becoming so old and run down."

"Well, yes, to people who live a long time."

"Will that happen to me?"

"If you have a long life, you too will eventually get old."

As a strong and vibrant twenty-nine-year-old, it was hard for Siddhartha to imagine that one day he would be old and weak.

Soon thereafter, they rode by an extremely sick man. He wasn't old, but he was quite ill.

"What is wrong with him?" Siddhartha asked the charioteer.

"He appears to be very sick."

"Can anyone be struck with illness like that?"

"Yes. It could happen to anyone."

More sobering news. When they passed a rotting corpse on the side of the road, flies were buzzing all around and the stench was horrid.

"How awful! Is that the smell of death? Does everyone die? Will that happen to me too?"

"Yes, Prince Siddhartha. That is the smell of a decomposing body, and eventually you will die too. No one lives forever."

Siddhartha's heart was heavy. As they began their trip back to the palace, another unusual sight caught Siddhartha's attention—a bald-headed man in a robe. Siddhartha had never seen someone dressed like that, nor had he seen a shaved head.

"Who is that?"

"He is an ascetic."

"What does that mean?"

"It means he has chosen to practice extreme self-denial as a way to achieve salvation."

Of the four revelatory sights Siddhartha encountered that day, he felt most encouraged by the ascetic. Having witnessed the ravages of old age, sickness, and death in the span of a few short hours, Siddhartha found comfort in the idea that he could practice a lifestyle aimed at reducing suffering.

Upon returning to the palace, Siddhartha immediately sought out his father. He found him in his bathroom, combing a dark substance through his hair.

"What are you doing, Father?"

"I am dyeing my hair. It is becoming gray, and I don't like it. I don't want to look old."

Siddhartha said, "You have hidden so much from me. Right outside the palace gates, there is tremendous suffering. How can we be of benefit when we turn our backs on the harsh realities of life?"

"I see you are upset, my son, but this needn't concern you. You've had a long day. Go get some rest. You'll feel better in the morning."

That night as he slept, Siddhartha received a powerful vision that he was supposed to leave the palace and become an ascetic. He awoke with absolute certainty about this. But as he prepared to leave, he received a message that his wife had just given birth to their first child, a baby boy. Siddhartha was the father of a newborn son! What a blessing, and what a dilemma.

Siddhartha felt an immense pull to leave life as he knew it, and he simultaneously felt drawn to begin a new chapter with his wife and raise their son together. He thought, "How can I possibly leave my wife and son now? That would be selfish. I would be considered the worst father ever. My father has done so much for me. Can I really abandon my child? I want so much to hold him."

As he looked in on his sleeping wife and son, Siddhartha wanted nothing more in that moment than to go to them. Then he thought, "How can I possibly stay here? That would be selfish. If I stay here because of my newborn son and wife, my focus will remain on my small, privileged world. It will be as if I never left the palace and saw what I saw.

I can't do that. I can't pretend I didn't see what I saw. If I go now, I can live in service to all children and spouses. I will meditate and pray every day in an effort to find the answers to end suffering."

With this first bold act of self-deprivation, Prince Siddhartha left the palace. Once he was well beyond the palace grounds, he cut his hair with his sword and changed from his royal garb into simple clothes. For the next six years, Siddhartha lived in the forest, committed fully to the ascetic life. He studied with five fellow ascetics and pushed himself mercilessly, enduring pain as he pit his mind against his body. Sometimes he subsisted on nothing more than one grain of rice a day. But no matter how hard he tried, he couldn't find the answers he sought.

He became emaciated. Too weak to study or meditate, he knew he'd die soon if he didn't obtain more nourishment. He also realized that extreme deprivation was no more a path to salvation than the life of luxury he had been raised in.

When a kind woman offered him some food, he gladly accepted. He told his five companions that he no longer believed their hard-core lifestyle would bear fruit, and that a life of balance made more sense. He was going to begin eating again and asked if they wanted to join him in creating a new path, a middle way. Criticizing him for selling out, they abandoned him.

Surrounded by no one else's dogma, and with his strength restored by food and drink, Siddhartha bathed in the river and returned to meditation. He spread out a mat of grass under a Bodhi tree, sat down, closed his eyes, and waited. He vowed not to get up until he received the truths he had long sought. He remained in a deep state of meditation for six days.

When he opened his eyes to the rising morning star, he realized that what he had been looking for had never been lost. There was nothing to attain and no more struggle to attain it. Infinite wisdom, peace, and contentment lay within him and always had. At the age of thirty-five, Siddhartha Guatama became Buddha, the Awakened One.

At first he was awed by the realizations and wasn't sure how best to convey them to others. For a few weeks he pondered this. Then he encountered a sage teacher who told him it was his duty to teach others now that he was the Awakened One. Shortly thereafter, Buddha arrived at Deer Park in Benaras and saw his five former companions. They wanted to ignore him because he broke his vows of extreme asceticism, but they couldn't help but notice how radiant he had become. They were curious about this profound change in him.

As they gathered around Buddha, he began to deliver the dharma, his teachings, for the first time. He said there are four noble truths that show the way to end suffering.

I've summarized the four noble truths here, followed by a simple way you can remember and work with each one when you are faced with a problem.

The Four Noble Truths

1. **Existence is suffering.**
   I recognize I have a problem.

2. **Suffering is caused by human craving.**
   What is the specific root of this problem?

3. **There is a cessation of suffering, which is nirvana.**
   Even if I don't see it right now, there is a solution to my problem.

4. **Nirvana can be achieved in this or future lives through the eightfold path of right views, right resolve, right speech, right action, right livelihood, right effort, right mindfulness, and right concentration.**
   There are specific steps I can take to address and resolve this problem. I just need to take the necessary steps.

Buddha's eightfold path offers eight guiding principles we can apply to our behavior and to better understand ourselves. Applying these eight principles requires that we balance the qualities of confidence, mindfulness, effort, concentration, and wisdom.

The relationship between the physical and spiritual is an important part of the balance we must maintain if we want to reduce suffering and enjoy happier, more peaceful lives. A balanced life is also what Buddha refers to as The Middle Way.

Balance is not the same as passivity. When you walk The Middle Way, you repeatedly choose thoughts and deeds that are most likely to create happiness. Buddhism itself is sometimes referred to as The Middle Way, since it seeks to reconcile opposing viewpoints and maintain balance.

Integrating Insight

1. Do you remember the first time you were away from home and witnessed a great suffering—something that surprised you because it was so different from anything else you had seen before? If so, what did you see, and how did it impact you?

2. How has enduring a huge loss changed your life for the better?

3. How will you bring more balance to your life?

Joy

28

Pure Generosity

THIS IS THE STORY of one of the best gifts I have ever received. It wasn't the biggest or fanciest gift, but at that time in my life, it felt like the best gift ever. I was in my twenties and living in Australia. It was a lovely summer day. As I waited outside for a friend to pick me up, I heard footsteps behind me. Next thing I knew, the person who belonged to those footsteps dropped a twenty-dollar bill in front of me. I was so happy!

Perhaps if you were sitting on the sidewalk and someone threw twenty dollars your way, you'd be embarrassed. Maybe you'd wonder, "Does that person think I'm homeless? Do I look like I'm homeless?"

That wasn't my reaction. As a monk, I am accustomed to receiving things. I went on daily alms rounds to accept donated food for my breakfast beginning at the age of eleven. But this gift was different for several reasons. First, I hadn't asked for it. Second, I hadn't expected it. It was a total surprise. And there's a third reason. As I looked up to say, "Thank you," no one was there.

No, this isn't about a mysterious angel or ghost. This story is about a real person. Looking down the block, I saw the back of the young man who had just gifted me twenty dollars. Since he was the only other person on that stretch of road, I knew he was the one responsible for this gift.

He didn't wait for my acknowledgment because he didn't need it. I'm guessing he saw a monk and decided in the moment to make a donation. I like to imagine that by making a donation to a monk on his way to work or wherever he was going, he felt good. He got everything he needed without being officially acknowledged for his generosity.

In Sri Lanka the word "giving" means "going away from the hand." I view this as the purest form of generosity—giving unconditionally, with zero need for recognition. That twenty-dollar bill was one of the greatest gifts I have ever received because the giver gave freely, without reservation or expectation. His was an act of pure generosity, and it was delicious.

* * *

In the story above, I was the fortunate recipient of pure generosity. In the next story, I was on the giving side of the equation, and the rewards were significant for everyone involved.

I was in Lima, Peru, having been invited back by the University of Virginia to teach meditation on a cruise ship as part of one of their special travel programs for alumni. A group of fellow passengers and I were enjoying a day trip. While they shopped, I relaxed in the sun.

Not far from where I sat, a shoemaker worked along the roadside. He appeared to be in his fifties, and I observed him toiling diligently under the hot sun. I was there for a considerable amount of time while my companions shopped, and I didn't see anyone visit the shoemaker's stand.

I decided I wanted to give him some money, but I didn't have any with me. My friend Michael was handling our cash that day. When Michael and the others met up with me again, I pointed to the shoemaker and said I wanted to give him money.

"Why do you want to do that?" Michael asked.

"I'm not sure, but it's something I want to do."

Michael was puzzled by my reply. Since he seemed hesitant, I added, "No need to ponder this so much. It just feels like the right thing."

Other companions chimed into the conversation.

"How much do you want to give?"

"Maybe twenty or thirty dollars. What do you think? Would you also like to contribute?"

In response to additional questions from the others, I simply said, "I don't know why I want to do this, but I do know I am experiencing it as a deep heart feeling."

"Well, that's good enough for us. Shall we take up a hat collection?"

Within a matter of moments, we had collected eighty dollars, and a member of our group who spoke Spanish offered to translate. We approached the shoemaker, introduced ourselves, and asked if we could chat with him for a few minutes. He nodded that we could, and we began to learn more. He told us about his three children and said he was very worried about what they'd eat for dinner because it was already late in the afternoon and he hadn't sold any shoes that day. There were tears in his eyes as he spoke. I could see how scared he was.

When we said we'd like to give him some money, he beamed. He probably thought we were going to give him a few dollars. When we handed over eighty dollars, his mouth opened wide in surprise. Tears of joy sprung from his eyes.

He told us how much our gift meant to him and how much it would help his family. Even though he said all this in Spanish, we didn't need our friend to translate because he was communicating so clearly. I realized this was because he was speaking from his heart. We had given from our hearts, and he had received our gift from his heart. It was a perfect exchange.

When we returned to the ship that evening, it was all my companions could talk about. We couldn't stop smiling as we shared how amazing we felt to connect with the lovely shoemaker. It was the highlight of our day.

I am sure you have heard that it is greater to give than receive. I think both can be wonderful. We had given relatively little, yet *without wanting or expecting it*, we received so much in return. Even now as I recall that day, I can feel the shoemaker's pain and stress about the lack of customers. I also can feel his relief upon receiving an unexpected gift.

Each one of us was affected by the shoemaker's joy. It was infectious. Together we experienced gratitude for one another and for the moment. We all became richer and more blessed that day.

Integrating Insight

1. List three of the favorite gifts you have ever received. Then list three of the favorite gifts you have ever given.

2. Do you enjoy giving and receiving equally? If not, why not?

3. Pay attention the next time you are either a giver or recipient. Are you able to give and receive from a place of pure generosity—from your heart and with no expectations?

29

The Key to Joy

THIS STORY IS ABOUT Mullah Nasruddin, who some say is a mythological character and others claim was a real person who lived in the thirteenth century. In this tale, Mullah Nasruddin has misplaced the key to his house. He cannot find it anywhere. He is down on his hands and knees on the sidewalk in front of his house, under a street lamp, searching frantically, when his friend approaches.

"I came to surprise you with a visit, Mullah. But I am the one who is surprised. I didn't expect to find you crawling around outside. Are you okay?"

"No, I am not. I lost my house key and I have been searching for it for hours."

"Please allow me to help you."

The friend got down on his hands and knees and began scouring the area. He couldn't find the key either.

"Do you recall where you last saw your key, Mullah?"

"Yes, inside my house."

"Then why are we looking out here?"

"Because the light is better here."

* * *

There are several kernels of wisdom in this silly tale. For starters, we often search for answers outside ourselves without understanding that the answers lie within. Mullah's house might represent ourselves and the missing key might represent whatever we're seeking—be it joy, peace, clarity, freedom, love, or something else altogether.

Another way to view the key is as an emotional or psychological tool. Have you ever heard the expression, "If you only have a hammer, everything looks like a nail"? The more psychological and spiritual tools we have, the better able we are to approach challenges skillfully, using the right tool in the right moment.

Nasruddin's missing key also could symbolize the concept of a magic solution. As if there is a magic answer "out there"—a missing key—and once we find it, everything in our life will automatically get better. Life is more nuanced than that. There is no external magic key, magic bullet, or magic anything that will suddenly make our worries vanish.

As much as we might desire immediate gratification, it is the slow and steady daily practice of cultivating the mind, deepening self-awareness, and behaving with compassion that paves the way for joy and peace. Our practice is the key.

Integrating Insight

1. What does Nasruddin's story mean to you?

2. What emotional comforts do you tend to seek outside yourself? Validation, approval, admiration, and love from others are a few examples of common things people look for outside themselves.

3. Now that you've identified some of your "tender areas" or vulnerabilities, how will you begin to rely on yourself for what you need?

30

Like Attracts Like

A LARGE GROUP OF MONKS were gathered with Buddha by Mount Vulture Peak when Sariputta, a senior monk known for great wisdom, stood up and began walking in large circles. Wordlessly, several other monks followed suit behind him. Shortly thereafter, Maha Moggallana, a senior monk known for his psychic abilities, walked a few feet in another direction and began his own walking meditation. He, too, attracted followers.

This continued with several more senior monks: Maha Kassapa, who usually lived alone in the forest and was known for his ascetic practice; Anuruddha, the clairvoyant one; Punna Mantani-putta, a skilled teacher and speaker; Upali, the Vanayi expert; and Ananda, Buddha's personal attendant. When each of these monks began doing a walking meditation, others joined them.

Buddha, who had been sitting under a tree observing this for a while, stood up and addressed the monks. He asked if they all noticed that Sariputta was pacing and being followed by others. When they nodded affirmatively, Buddha named each of the other senior monks and asked the group if they noticed that those monks also were doing walking meditations in large circles and that each one had attracted followers.

After the group acknowledged they noticed this as well, Buddha explained why this was happening. He said it was because of their qualities—their natural elements or characteristics. Each monk was attracted to the senior monk who had qualities similar to their own. For example, the especially wise monks walked with Sariputta. The monks with psychic powers were drawn to Maha Moggallana, and so on.

Have you heard the expression, "Birds of a feather flock together"? Buddha was teaching that here as well as something more.

The final circle was led by Devadatta. Devadatta often is described as an evil monk. His very existence raises questions about why Buddha ordained such a flawed man. Some say it is because Buddha didn't believe in bad people, only in poor choices, and he wanted to give Devadatta a chance to behave better.

I would add that Devadatta's presence in this sutta is a reminder that people (either before they change or if they don't want to change) can be a bad influence on others. I see this all the time. Drinking people hang out with other people who drink a lot. Drug addicts look for other drug addicts. I don't say this with judgment. It is human nature to be drawn to those who share similarities and affirm our behavior.

Buddha's teaching reminds us to choose our friends carefully. Also, by noticing the individuals and types of people we are attracted to, we can learn more about ourselves.

Taking it one step further, the more you cultivate qualities in yourself that you desire and admire, the likelier you are to attract people and circumstances that reflect those qualities. Not only do you become a beacon of goodness that shines for others, but you also are surrounded by the light and love of your fellow travelers.

This is a deeply nourishing and joyful way to live. This is my wish for you.

Integrating Insight

1. How does the "birds of a feather flock together" scenario play out in your own life?

2. When you think about the friends you feel closest to now, do they demonstrate qualities you admire and characteristics you are happy to share?

3. If not, what changes will you make with respect to certain relationships or within yourself?

Journeying Onward

SPREADING JOY IS AN ENDLESS JOURNEY. In my experience, spreading joy and helping people are one and the same. This begins with doing my own practice, then going out in the world and representing my best self and purest intentions. Beyond whatever I say verbally, it's the way I choose to show up for others that matters. Connection, understanding, and collective action are a few of the many blessings that flow from mindful interactions.

The distracted world we live in is a tremendous playground for spiritual practitioners. It's a playground filled with opportunities and challenges, hope and heartbreak. Although some spiritual practitioners seek to escape the modern world, I believe it's important that we learn how to live in this world that so needs our care.

While being of service brings me joy, not everyone feels this way. I know men and women who are dedicated to helping others but end up feeling disappointed, upset, mad, or rejected. They have many complaints. Whether or not they realize it, it's because their expectations aren't being met. They desire appreciation and recognition, and they're not getting enough. With their attention turned outward awaiting external validation for their good deeds, they don't fully enjoy the subtle but powerful internal rewards.

It is problematic to view good deeds as means to an end. For me, being of service is my deep honor and practice. It is that simple. If I see something to do, I do it. This is my work. This is why I am here. I love it.

Sometimes I picture myself as a lotus leaf. When raindrops fall on a lotus leaf, they don't stay there and they don't get absorbed. They simply drip down and off the flower. As a monk and a human being, I get rained on by the good and bad of life just like everyone else. Yet like a lotus leaf, I allow all of it to wash over me. I try not to cling to the good or the bad. Living this way is peaceful. It fills me with joy and the desire to share this joy with others.

I recently hosted a brother monk at my home for a couple of weeks. He is an intelligent man who has been struggling with personal challenges. The morning he was leaving to return to his home, he said, "Bhante, thank you for the magic of these last two weeks. How do you do it?"

"Do what? What magic?"

"I don't know how to explain it other than to say that just by being around you, I have picked up your joy. I feel like a different person inside. I now want to do for others what you have done for me."

"I haven't done anything. The joy you are feeling has been inside you all along. It is your own Buddha-nature. Your inner light. Still, it makes me happy to hear you are feeling wonderful and that you're inspired to share your joy and light with others."

"Yes, this is exactly what I want to do. Can you offer any advice?"

"Brother monk, I feel your joy as you speak. Because you are feeling it, so am I. You needn't think too hard about how to spread the joy. Just *be* the joy. When you *are* the joy, it naturally flows from all your words and actions."

* * *

Now I turn from my brother monk to you, dear reader. To begin with, thank you for coming on this journey of opening your toolbox with me. You may have noticed that the final section of this book is called "Journeying Onward" rather than "Conclusion." This intentional wording reflects the reality that the spiritual journey is ongoing. I sincerely hope I have helped you begin to tap more deeply into the spiritual tools and wisdom that live within you.

You are a unique being of light. If, like my brother monk, you want to bring your light more fully into the world, continue to look inside yourself through meditation and mindfulness. Then try to better understand your behavior, thoughts, personality, strengths, and weaknesses. Regularly practice loving-kindness to yourself and others.

You have all the tools within you—everything you need—to take care of yourself and the world. In every single moment, you have the power to feel more joy and spread more joy by understanding who you are and by being yourself.

As we journey onward together, I encourage you to:

* Keep your toolbox open.
* Bask in the treasures of your inner wisdom.
* Bring the full glow of your light into the world.

I bow to you in gratitude for traveling with me through these pages and inside yourself. May your journey be continually blessed.

Glossary

Anisamsa: Benefit.

Bhavana: Cultivation of the mind, contemplation, spiritual cultivation. When translated into English, this Pali and Sanskrit word is commonly referred to as meditation.

Bhikkhu: A fully ordained male monastic in Buddhism. A Buddhist monk.

Bhikkhuni: A fully ordained female monastic in Buddhism. A Buddhist nun.

Buddha-nature: The light inside each one of us. The possibility to be content. The ability to build upon our basic goodness and evolve.

Dhamma: Pali word for Buddha's teachings. Cosmic law and order.

Dharma: Sanskrit word for Buddha's teachings. Cosmic law and order.

Dukkha: The world of suffering and dissatisfaction. (Dukkha and samsara are the opposite of nirvana.)

Enlightenment: Supreme bliss.

Kamma: Pali word for action. It's the intentions we put into our actions that lead to favorable or unfavorable results.

Karma: Sanskrit word for action. It's the intentions we put into our actions that lead to favorable or unfavorable results.

Merit: A fundamental concept in Buddhist ethics, merit refers to a beneficial and protective force that accumulates as a result of good deeds, acts, or thoughts.

Merit-making: This practice of doing good deeds is believed to bring agreeable results, determine the quality of the next life, and contribute to a person's growth toward enlightenment. Merit is also shared with deceased loved ones in order to help them in their new existence.

Metta: Loving-kindness.

Metta-Bhavana: The development or cultivation of loving-kindness.

Nibbana: The Pali word for the condition of being freed from suffering and the cycle of rebirth. (Nibbana is the opposite of dukkha and samsara.)

Nirvana: The Sanskrit word for the condition of being freed from suffering and the cycle of rebirth. (Nirvana is the opposite of dukkha and samsara.)

Samsara: The endless cycle of birth, death, and rebirth. Samsara often is equated with the word dukkha, which is the world of suffering and dissatisfaction.

Sentient Beings: All living beings.

Sutra: The Sanskrit word for a teaching or lesson.

Sutta: The Pali word for a teaching or lesson.

Wounded Mind: The emotional damage we suffer as human beings.

About the Authors

Venerable Bhante Sujatha

Ordained as a Buddhist monk in his native Sri Lanka at the age of eleven, Venerable Bhante Sujatha is singularly focused on adding more love to the world. As Founder and Spiritual Director of Blue Lotus Buddhist Temple and Meditation Center in Woodstock, IL, Bhante leads a congregation and also teaches loving-kindness to people seeking the art of contentment worldwide.

Bhante gives more than 380 talks and guided meditations annually, for which he travels hundreds of thousands of miles, often going straight from the plane to a podium. He speaks at temples, churches, meditation centers, yoga studios, schools, and universities. Whether he is leading a small group retreat or consulting with corporate giants, Bhante teaches that love is the way and peace is a constant practice.

His humanitarian work spans the globe, and this tireless crusader sleeps a mere three or four hours a night.

In recognition for his incredible impact in spreading Buddhism in America, Bhante was awarded the highest honor within his lineage when he was named the Chief Sangha Nayaka of North America in 2013.

Bhante's approach to meditation is deep and simple, and he shares core Buddhist teachings in ways that are practical and easy to understand. A radiant, funny, and wildly energetic monk, Bhante helps people attain peace that can only be found in deep silence. www.bhantesujatha.org

Stacey Stern

Introduced to meditation at the age of eleven, Stacey Stern has always been drawn to exploring inner worlds. She is a writer, coach, and communication consultant who loves helping people access and articulate the clearest, truest vision of themselves and their work.

Stacey guides businesses and non-profit organizations to raise the bar for their internal and external communications, and she partners with dynamic leaders to coauthor books about personal and professional growth and spirituality.

Authentic to the core, Stacey brings her heart, mind, and integrity wherever she goes. www.staceystern.com